FEEL
NO
FEAR

Bela Karolyi

and

Nancy Ann Richardson

New York

FEEL

The Power, Passion,

NO

and Politics

FEAR

of a Life in Gymnastics

Library of Congress Cataloging-in-Publication Data

Karolyi, Bela.
    Feel no fear : the power, passion, and politics of a life in gymnastics / Bela Karolyi and Nancy Ann Richardson.—1st ed.
      p. cm.
    Includes index.
    ISBN 0-7868-8020-1
    1. Karolyi, Bela. 2. Gymnastics coaches—Biography.
I. Richardson, Nancy Ann. II. Title.
GV460.2.K37A3   1994
796.44'092—dc20
[B]   93-40449
                                        CIP

First Paperback Edition

10 9 8 7 6 5 4 3 2 1

Text design by Levavi & Levavi

Acknowledgments

Bela Karolyi

Many thanks to my family, Marta and Andrea, my dear friends, Geza Pozsar, Paul Ziert, Larry Parker, Bill Archer, and Andy McCraw, and all my gymnasts, especially Nadia, Mary Lou Retton, and Kim Zmeskal. You have filled my life's story with love and joy.

Nancy Ann Richardson

My thanks to Jane, Art, Susan, Spencer, and Mary Ann, for believing, and to Bela, for sharing his story with me.

Dedication

On my twenty-ninth wedding anniversary I made a tape recording for my wife, Marta. I sang her one of my favorite songs, "The Wind Beneath My Wings." I love that song because it reminds me of Marta. She has been the love of my life, my partner in both marriage and business, my inspiration, comfort, and lifeline. When I look back on my life, I realize that I never could have achieved all my goals if it hadn't been for Marta.

When I write the word *we* in my autobiography it means me and Marta. We have been a team our whole lives—from our first teaching and coaching positions, our tremendous triumphs with Nadia, our devastating losses of both our loved ones and our country, and our newfound lives in the United States. I cannot imagine another woman who could have handled the life Marta has lived with such calm and grace. In the most difficult of times, it was Marta who was the rock—the one who did not let emotion cloud her vision, the one who refused to give up.

The success of my athletic coaching career has been the success of *our* career. We are both coaches, and we are both highly qualified and well trained. Our success in gymnastics was based on two major factors. I provided the enthusiasm, the force, and the aggressive manner. Marta provided the self-discipline and consistency.

I do not recall one day in our lives when Marta did not fulfill the day's obligations. If a workout was scheduled, even if it was the day after the greatest party in the world, Marta would make sure we were at the gym the next morning at 7:00 A.M. I am not sure I could have been so disciplined on my own—in fact, I am sure I wouldn't have been. We could be suffering the deepest sorrow of our lives, yet Marta would ensure that the day's schedule would be kept. Considering the tremendous highs and lows that filled our life, Marta's discipline was beyond value.

I dedicate this book to Marta, because without Marta there would not have been a book. She has stood with me as we've lost our gymnasts, our schools, our daughter, and our livelihood. She has struggled at my side to learn the language of our new country, to bring our daughter to America, to find jobs when no one wanted us, to create our first gymnasium, to coach our first elite U.S. gymnasts, to fight for our rights and those of our students. Marta hasn't just been there for it all, she has been part of it all. This autobiography is her story, too.

Contents

FEEL

NO

FEAR

Prologue: Nadia?

"Where is Nadia?" Her teammates bent their heads and avoided my eye. "Hey guys, where is Nadia?" A little voice hesitantly answered, "Nicolae Vieru took her to the hospital early this morning because her wrist was inflamed."

Jesus Christ, what to do! We were in the gym with a half hour to go before the optional portion of the 1979 World Championships in Fort Worth, Texas. We were less than five-tenths behind the Russians—the closest we had ever come in the compulsory portion of a competition—and my star gymnast, the Olympic Champion, had been taken to the hospital for a scratch on her wrist that I had medicated and bandaged the previous night. Taken by Nicolae Vieru, the director of the Gymnastic Federation in Rumania—a man who historically had taken every opportunity to undermine my power and influence in gymnastics.

We had all worked so hard to get to this moment. Nadia was in the best shape of her life. A totally new Nadia, not the wisp of a girl she was in 1976, but a grown-up beautiful young lady—lean, tall, and performing skills that were unbelievable. We knew that the World Championships were going to be the stiffest competition we had faced, and did not break in our preparation.

A month before the competition, the team had flown to Mexico so the kids could adjust to a new time zone and climate. The Rumanian government had purchased American gymnastics equipment so our gymnasts could train on the same apparatus they would compete on a few weeks later. The kids were more than ready. Their preparation had been an everyday, continuous program—physical and technical preparation. They were flying. Routine after perfect routine. They could easily do five routines in a row without any mistakes in them. Six days before the competition we went to Fort Worth, Texas.

In Fort Worth we were calm and confident during our podium workouts. We watched the Russians, and they were excellent. I knew that there was going to be a fight between us for the gold, but I also knew that nobody had worked longer than we had. Our kids had more physical hours in their bones, more definition in their systems, and that meant we were going to be more consistent than any other team.

After the compulsories we were trailing the Russians by only five-tenths of a point. The night before the optional competition I lined up the kids and gave my final speech. I said, "Tomorrow, competition time, will be absolutely normal. Watch your expressiveness, let the people enjoy your talents. Show your capabilities and let your face show you are a gymnast who enjoys herself out on the floor. Show your joy and confidence to the people." The kids were excited. I remember that I said to Nadia that tomorrow was her big day. She was in the greatest shape of her life. Just be confident, I said, and show the world what you can do.

Nadia didn't need encouragement. She had never been more perfect. She did have a scrape on her wrist, a skin irritation from the rub of the equipment, but we never paid too much attention to those small things. Before Nadia went to bed that night, I put some antibiotic cream on her wrist and a small bandage. It was the same as always, when Nadia needed a little medical attention, or a little massage for her sore muscles, I took care of it. For nine years I had successfully taken care of Nadia's needs.

"Where is Nadia?" It didn't matter at that moment. With five gymnasts left, and less than fifteen minutes before the optional competition began, we had to continue our practice workout. The Russians had already observed our turmoil. They didn't know what had happened, but they knew that Nadia was not on the floor.

I split up the kids and Marta took half to the beam while I worked with the others on the bars. Suddenly I saw one of the kids turn. "Sir, Nadia is at the door." I looked toward the doorway. There was Nadia, standing next to Vieru. Nadia looked into my eyes and held up her hand. It was enormous, bandaged in a huge white wrap. I looked at Vieru. He was smiling.

I walked to Nadia and told her to get her leotard on. She looked at me. I said it again, "Get your leotard on"—there was never a question of not following my directions. Nadia went to the bench and took off her coat, jacket, and pants. She was already wearing her leotard. She had been ready for the competition when Vieru had come to take her to the hospital.

"Nadia," I said, "go to the parallel bars and begin your practice routine." Nadia began to work on the bars with one hand. I told her to grab the bar with both hands and she said, "Sir, I can't do it. I can't hold it; my hand is numb." "What did they do to you, Nadia?" I asked. "What in the world did they do to you?" "They cut my wrist and put stitches in," she began. "I didn't know what was going on, and I could not say a thing. They gave me an injection and knocked me out. Vieru said they were just going to clean it a little bit to get me in better shape."

I looked over at the Russians. They were celebrating—hugging and shaking hands. I mean, you could see it from an airplane, the blood coming through Nadia's bandage. The Russians were certain that they had already won. I looked at my remaining team—five terrified kids who had lost their leader. A team that had always been so comfortable performing because the big responsibility never fell on their shoulders. The big responsibility always fell on Nadia. I knew I had to turn the situation around.

But I am getting ahead of myself. It is so difficult to know where to start—there is so much I want to tell. So I will follow what a particularly American phrase dictates: I will begin at the beginning.

1.

Dracula

I never knew Dracula. It wasn't until I came to America that I learned that vampires were supposed to inhabit my homeland—sleeping by day in coffins and sucking the blood of unsuspecting townspeople by night. I had never heard of Dracula, but as a child, I was familiar with the stories about Vlad Tepes—his popular name was Vlad Dracul, the Prince of Wallachia.

Vlad Tepes was a cruel, sadistic fifteenth-century Rumanian prince. His nickname, Dracula, meant "son of the devil," and his surname, Tepes, meant "impaler"—his favorite form of punishment, second only to skinning and boiling his victims. In many languages the word *devil* is interchangeable with the word *vampire*, thus the legend.

But legends were not the stuff of my childhood. My childhood memories are of the beauty of my homeland. My grandparents lived in one of the poorest areas of Transylvania—a small coal mining town in the middle of the Carpathian mountains. It was one of the most beautiful places in the world—a high plateau circled by a granite ring of snow-covered peaks. It was not just the mountains that made the entire plateau, known as Transylvania, beautiful. It was the sheer geographic diversity—the rivers and streams, the woods and wildflowers.

My grandfather was a life-loving Hungarian; he liked parties, good wine, and pretty women. He was also the very first teacher in his village of Vulcan, a legendary person. It was said that he was the one who "brought the light to the people." Generations were not only educated by him, they were also entertained by him. Grandpa was always organizing musical shows and soap opera–like plays for the miners and their families. There was nothing else going on in Vulcan, just some small houses, dirt streets, and a few beer joints, so his efforts were greatly appreciated.

My grandmother, a very German lady, was the opposite of my grandfather. She was a strict, rigid disciplinarian, a powerful matri- arch who dominated the entire family. We were never fooled by the fact that she looked like a picture-perfect grandmother, all sweetness with white hair and sparkling eyes. No, no one could ever do anything right by her standards. My father's sisters never married because my grandmother told them their obligation in life was to care for her. She set all the rules, and you either followed them or went to Hell.

Following World War I, the mining town where my grandparents lived started to industrialize. Machines replaced the men in the mines and many men, looking for easy work, moved to the area. The crime rate increased and the basic social life that my grandfa- ther loved started to disappear. Liquor stores and bars changed the entire face of the village, and my grandfather knew he could no longer live in Vulcan. In addition, the conflict between his person- ality and my grandmother's had been brewing for many years. The situation became unbearable, and he finally left. After he moved to a quieter area of Transylvania, he sent for the family. He desperately wanted us to come to him, but we never did.

I was born in 1942, and have few memories of my grandfather— save my father telling me to stay away from him. But I loved my grandfather very much, and remember that whenever I was with him the world seemed light. Later in my life I talked to the old people who knew him and learned that our personalities were very similar. He was always active, restless, and used his energy to do things for others. He loved life, and he was a fighter. I wish I could have spent more time with him. I wish we could have known each other. I think he would have appreciated my personality. I know that he would have been proud of me.

When I was a boy, my family lived in the town of Cluj, the capital of Transylvania. My father was a civil engineer. He was a disciplined, stern man who was much like his mother. He was consistent in his work and in his life, but he was rooted to the ground. My mother did not have much of a personality. She never complained, and she never stood up for anything in her life. She was an accountant during the day, and she took care of the family at night.

My sister, Maria, was the apple of my father's eye. The first thing he did when he returned home from work was ask her how her day had been. He idolized her because she was the brain in the family. Maria is two years older than me, and she was an extremely bright student. She finished high school when she was fifteen years old and immediately began studying to be a civil engineer like our father. By the time she was twenty-one, she had earned her degree. To be so young and to earn that type of a degree was unbelievable— it was the ultimate recognition of her brilliance.

I, on the other hand, had less interest in school. I hated math and science, and did everything in my power to avoid my home-work. And I got into trouble all the time. When I was young it was the animals. I began by raising pigeons, and then moved on to lambs. Then I started trying to sneak three or four dogs at a time into the house. The dogs were big, hairy, smelly things, and I was always caught, which always led to a fight. But I didn't care about getting into trouble, because I loved animals. I never tried to train them, I loved them as little beings. The second thing I got into trouble for was sports.

In sports I found a necessary ingredient for my life—the opportunity to be a winner. I wasn't a very talented child, but I won in sports because I worked harder than the other kids. I never complained if somebody beat me, I just squeezed my teeth and said to myself, next time I will be more prepared. Next time I'm gonna win. That ethic reappeared in my coaching years later. As a coach I never worried about the final product, I always focused on the preparation. I knew from my years as a competitive athlete that the best prepared person always won.

My first competitive sport was track and field. I was a bulky child, way bigger than the other fellows, and heads taller than the rest of my class. I figured that I could do well in a sport where not too many people were involved, a sport where my size would be an advantage. I began to compete in the hammer throw.

At first I didn't do well—I had no idea how to prepare, how to train, or how to throw. I decided that hour after hour of practice, even if I wasn't doing everything exactly right, was the answer. I spent my thirteenth winter teaching myself how to hammer throw on the outskirts of my town. For hours I'd swing and twist. It was a very primitive type of preparation. I had no coach, but I knew that I had to keep swinging and throwing, and gradually, I became more skillful. That spring I won the school hammer throwing championship. I was the most satisfied person in the world.

Following the championship, I met a man, a local fellow, who was the best hammer thrower in town. He told me that I needed to train with weights to increase my strength, and he showed me a few different techniques. Later, he became my first coach. As a result of his supervision, by the time I was fourteen I was a member of the national hammer throwing team. I set the national record for distance. This record stood for many years—partly because the weight of the hammer was changed from 6 kilograms (13.2 pounds) to a more popular 7.235 kilograms (15.9 pounds). No matter, I still remember the sense of bursting pride that I felt on the day I made that record. And regardless of my father's disapproving glares, that feeling was never tarnished.

Pride, a sense of fulfillment, and the respect of my peers continued to guide my athletic activities as I grew older. It was in high school that I joined the handball team and had my first team coach. Our coach was also the track coach, and he had many other athletes to train. Consequently, the team was pretty much on its own as far as training. Since we had little guidance, we focused on preparation—hours more than any other team. As a result, we were the team handball champions for four consecutive years. Later in my life I learned to appreciate the value of specialized coaches. It is so important to have someone to guide your steps and eliminate unnecessary frustrations. It is also vital to have someone cheer your hard work, and give you a hug or a pat on the head.

My father never came to see me compete. He was not interested in any type of athletics. My mother spent her afternoons preparing the family meal, and she would never have come to watch me or cheer my efforts. Because of that, I have tried very hard during most of my coaching career to give that kind of parental petting and attention to the kids. I have always wanted them to have what I needed and never got.

My father considered me the black sheep of the family because of my interest in sports and my disinterest in mathematics, part of our family's tradition. There were many arguments. Still, I remember those years as a beautiful time. A quiet, smooth time where riding my bike to practice and playing with the animals dominated my life.

I did, however, have a dream other than success in competitive sports: I wanted to become a veterinarian. But that opportunity was far removed from my reality. Becoming a veterinarian involved a lot of money. It also involved passing extremely difficult entrance exams. In addition, I didn't have a good enough political background, which in Rumania meant that your parents were heavily involved in the politics of the Communist party. While my father wasn't anti-government, he was not considered pro-government. So I was never going to be a veterinarian. Instead, I hoped to go to college to study physical education. That dream was one my father neither knew of at the time nor would have approved of.

On the last day of high school I took my graduation exam. Passing the exam meant that I would receive a high school diploma; failing the exam meant no diploma. I wasn't sure how I would do—I felt I was weak in the sciences. My abilities in history, literature, and languages, however, balanced that weakness. Following the exam the officials immediately announced who had passed. My name was on the list.

When I arrived home my mother had prepared a festive dinner to celebrate my graduation. My father came home and gave me his congratulations. We sat down to dinner. "Bela," my father began, "I am very proud of you. You messed around a lot in high school, wasted a lot of time with your sports, but I still have a surprise for you." My father said he would tell me the surprise after dinner. The tension during the rest of the meal was almost unbearable. I had the feeling something bad was about to happen.

"Bela, tomorrow morning you are to show up at the engineering institute where I work; you are going to begin classes in mathematics and physics with an assistant from the institute. Next week you will take the entrance exam for the school of engineering. I have worked very hard, very hard, to give you this opportunity." My father looked at me expectantly—he was waiting for my thanks.

It was a heartrending situation. I didn't want to disappoint my father, or hurt him. I had felt like the outcast of the family my whole life, the one who was not what my father wanted. I wanted him to be proud of me, just as he was proud of my sister.

I knew that I could not go to the institute the next morning—I had to leave for the Balkan track and field championships. Success in those championships might have provided me with scholarship money to attend a physical education school. I also knew that I would not be a good engineer—I had no drive or desire to spend the rest of my life working with numbers and scientific methods. My father kept talking. "Okay, Bela," he continued, "you must be at the institute at ten A.M. . . ." I interrupted him. "I cannot be there, I have a track meet and we are leaving tomorrow." My father was furious. *"I have worked very hard to give you this opportunity, I have set everything up. You have had enough time to play, forget the play now, it is time to work hard and study."* My father never accepted anyone in the family saying no to him. I said no.

That dinner was the first celebration in my honor that my family had ever held. By the time the evening ended, I had been disowned by my father and kicked out of his house. My mother cried as I packed my things. She begged me not to leave, but I had no choice. I could not do what my father had asked.

As I walked out the door of my parents' home, I had no idea where to go. I headed to the sports stadium and slept there. The next morning I left for my competition. When I returned two weeks later I could not go home. It was the same town, but I no longer had a home in it. No home, no job, no money, and no family. I have never felt such an emptiness.

2.

Homeless

As a homeless seventeen-year-old, I knew two things: one, I needed a warm place to sleep, and two, I needed money so I could eat.

I applied for athletic housing at the sports stadium—housing was offered to athletes on the track and field team. My application was approved. Now I had a bed, but I still needed money. I had to find a job. A friend suggested that I apply for a job at the slaughterhouse. He told me that working at the slaughterhouse was great, because all I'd have to do is clean, lift, and carry things. I could also hide meat in my pocket at the end of the day so that I'd have dinner. The next day I applied for the job.

For three weeks I cleaned, loaded, and unloaded trucks. One day it was so cold, so damn cold, that I snuck into the slaughterhouse to get warm. The *meszaros* (professional butchers) were hard at work, and I tried to hide in a corner. "Hey, do you know who that guy is," asked a man next to me. He was pointing to an enormous middle-aged butcher working to our left. I told him I had no idea. "That's Jeno Doda Bacsi, the great boxing coach." My God, I had heard so much about the great Doda. He had been the European Heavyweight Boxing Champion—he was legendary. I was a big kid for my age, and fairly muscular, for that reason I believe I attracted Doda's attention.

"Hey, boy, do you want something to eat?" Doda asked me. It was lunchtime and everyone was eating—I was so hungry I was dying. "Yes, sir," I said, "thank you very much, I would love to eat." Doda gave me a big piece of meat and we began to talk. He asked my age, and then he asked whether I wanted to work inside the slaughterhouse. I was thrilled. "Hey, boy, you're built strongly, have you ever boxed?" I told him no. "Well, I am going to teach you how," he said.

At the end of the day, Doda and I walked to his boxing gym. "Are you afraid of anything?" Doda asked. "I never really thought about being afraid," I said. "Has anybody ever hit you real hard?" "Well, my father beat me a few times, but other than that, no," I said. We stopped outside the door to the gym. Doda looked at me very seriously and said, "Listen boy, you have to fight here, because if you don't hit somebody, then they will hit you hard as hell."

Doda and I hit the punching bag for a while. Then he told me to get in the ring with another guy. Before we began to box, Doda said, "Don't forget, if you don't hit him, he'll hit you." The guy I faced was no bigger than me, but he was well built. I didn't know at the time that he was the regional boxing champion. He came at me and *bam, bam, bam* he hit me three times in a row. My eyes were watering, my nose was bleeding, but he just kept hitting. I said to myself, I better hit this sucker. Doda was right, the moment I stopped throwing punches that guy was all over me. By the time the bell rang I could no longer breathe through my nose. My eyes were so swollen I had trouble seeing, and blood was everywhere.

"Go wash yourself, boy," Doda commanded. For the next hour

Doda showed me how to fight. He taught me direct punches, jabs, and body movement. When it was over, I left the gym and walked back to the stadium. I had missed my afternoon workout, and had to tell my coordinating coach that I had been in a fight. The next morning I returned to the slaughterhouse, and to my new coach, Doda.

The ensuing months were a blur. I was exhausted. I would walk four miles to the slaughterhouse, work all day lifting and carrying heavy boxes, walk five miles to the boxing gym and get beat up, then walk five more miles to the stadium for my sport workout. I could not drop any activity. I needed money to eat, I needed Doda to provide me with a warm and secure job inside the slaughterhouse, and I needed the stadium for a place to live, which meant practicing with the track and field team. Also, in the back of my mind was a desire to go to college for a physical education degree. I had to excel in athletics if I had any hope of a scholarship.

After several months of boxing, Doda decided I was ready for my first competitive fight. My first boxing match was a regional competition. I made it to the finals, and in order to win I had to fight the animal who beat me up that first day in the gym. I was a bit scared of him—first impressions are always very strong. I knew that I had the basic instruction needed to put up a good fight, but Doda had not put us in the ring together since that first day. I didn't know what to expect. I thought maybe I'd get beaten badly again. We had a clean match, no knockouts and no clear victor. In the end, however, I won by points. I had qualified for the zone meet.

I began to train intensively. I rescheduled my track and field practices. Now, I returned from boxing at 8:00 P.M. and then trained for the next three hours in track and field.

The Zone Boxing Championship was held over the summer. A week before the meet, after months of neither seeing nor contacting my family, my aunt and my godmother found me at the sports stadium. They had been searching for me for months. They were worried about me, and they wanted me to come home. My aunt (my father's sister) was a unique woman. She was a dominating person like my grandmother, but she also had a bit of Grandpa in her. My godmother was also quite remarkable, and the two old ladies were great detectives.

So they found me, and when they discovered that I was boxing they went nuts. "Somebody will hurt you, oh, my God, somebody is going to beat you up," they cried. I promised them that I was just boxing as part of a job, and that I would never get involved with any kind of competition. I didn't know then that there were posters going up all over Transylvania for the Zone Championship. I just kept practicing with Doda until it was time for the championship, and hoping in the back of my mind that the old ladies would never discover the truth.

When the last match of the Zone Championship was called, the match between Paul Blass and Bela Karolyi, I heard some suspicious voices among the cheers from the crowd. I was fired up, so I didn't pay too much attention. The bell went off and we began the fight. That sucker got me right away—a real hard punch in my nose that started me bleeding. But I wasn't in any difficulty, and we kept on boxing. Paul got some good hits, I got some good hits, the match was going well. I heard Doda yelling, "Good boy, go get him, use your left jab. . . ." Then Paul hit me full force and my nose just burst up with blood. I heard two voices shrieking above the crowd and I knew those voices all too well.

"We're gonna kill that son of a gun. Don't you beat up our boy. . . ." I turned around and saw my godmother and my aunt swinging their umbrellas and hitting the organizers. They were big ladies, and the organizers were covering their heads and backing away. The embarrassment!

The bell sounded and the round was over. I turned to Doda and begged him to do something. Doda went over to my aunt and godmother and asked them to stop yelling. My aunt turned her umbrella on Doda and got in some good hits.

When the second round began I knew that I had better get the match over with quickly or I would die of embarrassment. I closed my ears and cornered my opponent with long and steady hits. In thirty seconds he was out cold.

I had earned the right to go to the National Boxing Championships in Bucharest. I was also traveling to Bucharest for the National track and field championships. I had my hat in two different rings. This was probably my last chance to win a scholarship to a physical education university, and I was trying every avenue possible. But I had to be careful. If the stadium people found out that I was boxing, I would lose my housing and maybe a chance at the scholarship.

The day before the final boxing match my cover was blown. A Bucharest newspaper published an article about me. They wrote about how I had upset the regional champion and that I was a finalist at the Nationals. They also wrote about my hammer throwing record, and that I was a member of the national track and field team. It was nice to get so much attention, but I was afraid I would lose everything. Yet none of my coaches were upset with me; instead, they applauded my efforts.

On the night of the big boxing finals all of my teammates from the different sports showed up to support me. I was so nervous. Just let me have a good fight, a wise fight, I thought. I don't care if I win, but I want to be careful and not get knocked out, to have a good technical fight. The first round went well, I got my opponent's advantage the second round, and I dominated the third round. In the end I was named the Junior National Boxing Champion. It was a big night for me.

The next day I got an offer from one of the largest steel mills in the country. The mill was located in Hunedoara, and they had a huge boxing and track and field team. They wanted me to join their union club—a club with a lot of money and power. I accepted the offer, hoping to eventually get a college scholarship from the mill. I had no belongings, so I did not return to Cluj, but moved immediately to Hunedoara. I worked in the steel mill in the mornings and spent the afternoons training.

Things did not go well. I did not progress in either sport. There was too much free time, and I was used to a very strict schedule. In addition, I hated my job because it was not physical work, mostly just killing time for five or six hours. When no scholarship was offered, I started to save money for college. I was desperate to save money, and I began to skimp on food. The factory gave us meal tickets, but I sold my tickets and put the money aside for school. My physical condition deteriorated.

I got sick. At first it was the flu, then bronchitis, and then pneumonia. I didn't go to the doctor because that cost money. I was ready to give up—I had no energy, it had been eaten up by my constant fever. I was ready to die. I don't know how in the world they did it, but one day my aunt and my godmother were at my bedside. They had found me again! They took me home to Cluj.

My mother cried on my shoulder. Other than that, things were pretty normal at home. No reproaches. My father, feeling guilty about my illness, asked me if I still wanted to go to college. When I said yes, he said that there was a late admissions test being held at our town's technical college, which offered art and physical education programs. But there was a hitch: The late admission wasn't for the physical education program, but for the art school. "Want to try anyway, Bela?" my father asked.

The next morning I was down at the college getting information. I was told that in ten days an admissions test was to be held for four places in the school. Seventy-eight people had already signed up for the test; I became the seventy-ninth. I asked what the test involved. There were two days of oral tests in anatomy, history, literature, and language and then two major practical tests—one was clay sculpting and the other was painting. I had never in my life even drawn a dog.

There was no way, absolutely no way. I couldn't paint, and even though I'd played with clay as a kid, I had never made anything recognizable. I knew that I was going to fail; still, I tried. I took the oral exams, which were 70 percent of the entry score. I couldn't believe my eyes when I saw my name posted in third place after the exam. Once again my abilities in history, literature, and language had helped me. There were four places open to students—I had a chance.

I bought some clay and took it home to practice sculpting. Nothing came out of that lump of gray. I asked my godmother if she knew any artists in town who could help me become a painter and sculptor in two days. She suggested that I go to see Dodi Lovasz, a local artist, famous ski racer, and later my brother-in-law. "Dodi, please teach me how to sculpt and paint," I begged. "Bela," he said, "it's not like literature, you can't memorize it, you have to have a hand for it. But if you'd like, I will try to show you a few things."

Lovasz told me about painting. He said that for the test I was most likely going to have a vase of flowers or an apple or pear that I would have to paint. He said that I should not try to paint what I saw, but what I didn't see. What? He told me that everything was made of shades. . . . My God, I didn't see any shades!

The morning of the painting exam arrived. All of the prospective students were given a block of paper, paint, and pencils. We were told to paint a vase and an apple. I looked around and everyone was sketching the vase and apple with their pencils. I tried to sketch the objects but had no luck. I looked around again, and all the other people were walking up to the vase and apple and looking at them very closely, with their eyes squinted, and then returning to their desks to paint. I figured I might as well look important, so I walked closer to the objects and stared at them, too. But when I returned to my desk I wasn't any smarter.

Sitting next to me was a little girl who was painting furiously. She was very good. I whispered, "Excuse me, but I have never done a painting before in my life, could you help me?" She smiled and told me to pass my paper to her. I snuck my paper to the girl as the assistants walked through the row in front of me. *Swish-swash*, she sketched the objects and then handed me back my paper. "That's basically the drawing," she said, "now just fill in the colors." Fill it up? Okay. An assistant passed by and looked at my paper. He said my drawing was good.

"Hey," I whispered to the girl, "how exactly do I fill in the colors?" She told me to put gray here and there. . . . I filled in the colors, and I felt very important because I was doing what all the other students were doing. Finally the exam ended and I handed in my painting. It was still very primitive-looking, but at least I had completed the exam.

There were no results posted when we entered the classroom the next morning to take the sculpting exam. I saw the little girl who helped me and thanked her. "Can I sit next to you again?" I asked. She said yes. I pushed through the crowd so we would not get separated. For the next forty-five minutes I pummeled and poked at my mound of clay. I couldn't do a damn thing—the only thing I'd ever made out of clay was a coil ashtray. I looked over at the little girl, she was almost done. "Can you help me with this?" I asked. She took my clay.

Chop, chip, chop. The little girl made a statue of a man for me. She handed my clay back as all the big shots from the Art Institute walked through the doorway. "Just put in the lines under the eyes and cheeks," the girl whispered. I started to put in lines as the big shots passed by my desk. A woman stopped and said that my sculpture was very interesting. She asked me my name, and then she told me that I had an "interesting vision."

I turned to my little friend after the woman walked away and told her that I was sorry I had received attention, but that I thanked her very much. She smiled, and then helped me put the rest of the lines on my sculpture. Bless her heart, she was still willing to help me.

When the exam ended I did not expect ever to see the inside of that school again. I said goodbye to the teachers and went out to look for a job. I became very depressed. A few days later, I was having lunch when my sister came home and asked me how many students the college was going to take. I told her only four. "Then you made it," she said. "What do you mean, I made it?" I asked. She told me that I was the fourth name on the list that the college had posted.

I flew down to the college. There was a list, but it didn't have any scores on it. I went into the administration office and a secretary there told me that the people on the list were placed in order of their scores. "Does that mean that if I am fourth on the list I have made it into the school?" I asked. "You bet," she answered. I jumped up and down like I had lost my mind. I hugged the lady and ran out to tell everyone I knew. I was going to college.

3.

School Days

I knew that it was only a matter of time before I was expelled. I did not belong in art school. The little girl who had helped me paint and sculpt had not been accepted into the program, although she was obviously much more qualified than I. The only explanation I could find for her absence was that perhaps she had not scored well on the oral exams. Without that little girl, there was no one to cover for my lack of ability. It was a horrible feeling to stand before a sheet of paper and try to paint while my instructors clucked their tongues and shook their heads at my efforts. "Bela Karolyi, you have no natural talent. You do not belong here," they told me. I tried to smile, thank them for their comments, and explain that I appreciated their honesty but preferred to continue to try. But I wasn't fooling anyone, not even myself.

I had to find a way to get transferred into the physical education school of the college, so I made an appointment to see the dean. My only chance was to tell him the truth and hope that my past athletic accomplishments would carry some weight. "Sir, I can't paint, draw, or sculpt," I began. "I have no artistic ability and I do not belong in art school. I am an athlete, a boxer, rugby and handball player, and a hammer thrower. I belong in the physical education school." "Bela," he responded, "you are a famous track and field athlete, but we don't need big shots in our school. We need people who are dedicated to becoming educators," the dean explained. I told him that was what I wanted to be. "Then I will put you on the official waiting list," the dean said. There were five names on the list ahead of mine. My heart sank; by the time they reached my name I would have long been expelled from the art college.

I was lucky. Two people on the transfer list dropped out of college, another was transferred to a different school, and the fourth changed his mind. My name was now first on the list, and five weeks after my meeting with the dean I was transferred to the physical education school. I had finally made it; however, classes had already begun, and I was far behind. How was I going to catch up? Between my college handball team practices and competitions, and my responsibilities to the rugby team, which had given me some scholarship money for college, I didn't even have time to attend all of my classes.

I needed someone's notes. One day I looked around my class and noticed that the girl sitting next to me was taking great notes—I mean neat, organized, perfect notes. "Excuse me, can I borrow your notes?" I asked the girl. "Yes," she replied, "but please return them to me. They are the only thing I can learn from, because the books are too expensive for me to buy."

That week I had a competition, and I forgot all about the girl and her notes. Several days later she approached me. "You forgot to return my notes," she said. "Oh, gosh, I am so sorry," I said, and I tore through my bag to find them. I handed her back her notes, slightly crumpled. I apologized again. As she walked away I thought, that's the last time I'll get notes from her.

I continued to miss several classes each week. Before I knew it oral exams week had begun, and I had no notes to study from. I had nothing to lose, so I turned to the girl in my class. "Excuse me, but could I please, please, borrow your notes? I will never, ever, forget to return them again." She gave me her notes, I returned them on time, and I passed my oral exams. For the next few weeks I continued to skip classes and borrow the girl's notes.

The dean caught me sneaking out of a lecture one afternoon. "Bela, don't run in four directions or you will catch no bird," he warned. "Stay within the school and take what we offer you. Physical education is a good career, a beautiful profession. Look forward to becoming an educator, not a vagabond." I thought about what he had said, and in my heart I knew he was right. I had to commit myself to becoming an educator—it was time for me to move forward with my life. I had never before had a teacher who made a big impression on me. But that man was different, his words rang true. The next day I bought my schoolbooks, cut my athletic practices short, and began to attend every class full-time.

I excelled in school. There was a sense of satisfaction in doing well that I had never before experienced. I was studying topics that really interested me, and I wanted to learn. It was deeply satisfying. The girl in my class still gave me her notes, but I was no longer asking for them because I needed them. I was asking so I could talk to her.

The curriculum of the physical education school did not involve just textbooks and lectures. We had practical classes—track and field, tennis, swimming, gymnastics, and so on. In order to pass each of our courses, we had to master every sport. Failure to pass the physical examinations in swimming, track and field, and gymnastics meant you were out of the college. Many of the sports I had never tried before, but I enjoyed learning new skills and progressed rapidly—except for gymnastics.

On the first day of gymnastics class we were lined up on a large mat. Our professor, also the dean of the school, taught us basic turns and movements. Then it was time for the tumbling portion of the class. After doing repeated forward rolls I was dizzy and sick to my stomach. Handstands were even worse. I was a big man, 130 kilograms (286 pounds) at the time, and I was so off-balance. My hands trembled and my head pounded from the rushing blood. Every time I went into a handstand—*phhhht*—I collapsed against the wall, hit my head, hit my ears, twisted my neck. I was embarrassed and frustrated. The dean told me that I had better work on my skills or I was going to fail the gymnastics examination.

Day after day I practiced those damn rolls, forward and backward, handstands, cartwheels, high bar, pommell horse. There were no organized practices so I had to learn on my own. Gradually I started to feel more confident, but I knew I still wasn't up to the requirements of the final examination. We were given a preliminary test, where we had to fulfill certain lower requirements before the final. I failed.

I was desperate. I had to find a way to pass the final exam. I went to the gymnasium during the gymnastic team's practice and tried to find someone to coach me. One of the assistants approached me and told me I couldn't practice while the team was using the gym. I explained that I really needed some help. He said that if I helped him spot the gymnasts on the women's team, he would help me after their practice. I looked over and saw Marta, the girl whose notes I had been borrowing. I was going to enjoy spotting the women's team!

With the help of the assistant coach, I managed to pass my final gymnastics examination. Most importantly, I had developed a love of the sport. By the second year of school I was attending regular gymnastics workouts with the college team. I had given up all my other sports and was concentrating solely on gymnastics. Toward the end of the year I made the team and started to compete. Unfortunately, in the second year of my competitive season I had an accident on the horse and broke my arm badly. I was set back physically, so I turned my total focus onto my schoolwork, and the results were positive.

That year I was elected the president of the student union, something I never thought would happen in my life. For the first time, I had become one of the most appreciated ones, a top student recognized by my peers and my professors. I began to teach introductory classes to the first year students, and to assist my professors. I also became very good friends with Marta.

Following my injury, I worked hard to get back into physical shape. My cast was off, and I had to get my arm strong. My vision, however, had shifted. I no longer had a serious interest in my own competitive gymnastics; I was now thinking of becoming a coach for gymnasts. I began to imagine how I was going to organize the kids, the challenge of coaching, and what I would do with my team. I wanted to be a good coach, to get something great out of my students, something different and unique.

After four challenging years graduation day arrived. I had such a sense of fulfillment. I had worked so hard for that day, and I had come so far both personally and professionally. I had direction, goals, and a future.

Marta Eross graduated first in our class. I graduated second. We had been dating for two years, and we planned to get married. The only decision we had to make was where we would work. Following graduation, the entire physical education community met in Bucharest at a large gymnasium where all of the education positions in the country were posted on the walls. Since Marta and I had graduated at the top of our class, we had the opportunity to choose our positions first.

We had to find two positions in the same town. There was no

way we were willing to be separated. I saw a position in my home-town, but there was only one spot available. Then I saw a posting for Vulcan, the coal mining area where my grandparents had lived. There was only one position available, but there was also a posting for Lupeni, which was only 6 kilometers (3.6 miles) away.

I was afraid Marta was going to say no. The positions were in the poorest part of Rumania. Our schools would not have money for equipment, and our salaries would be low. I turned to Marta and asked whether she would consider the coal mining towns. "We would be near each other?" she asked. I told her we would be very close. "Then let's take them, Bela," she replied.

The commission was very surprised when Marta and I turned our requests in. We had the choice of the biggest towns, the largest clubs. We had chosen the poorest area in the entire country. "Hey, what happened to you guys," the commissioners asked, "do you have a special interest in that part of the country?" We told them we had no special interest, we just wanted to be together. Our requests were accepted, and Marta went immediately to Lupeni where I was to join her after I fulfilled my country's six-month army obligation.

4.

A Great Punishment

The greatest punishment for a free spirit is to be forced to serve time in the army. In Rumania, every male had to serve for three months following college graduation. I considered the army the ultimate destruction of human personality, and every portion of my body was against everything about it. However, when I graduated from college, I, like all other college graduates, was forced to spend three months of officer training at an assigned army center.

I arrived at the base late in the evening. I told the guards there that I was a recruit, and they sent me to a building to get my military clothing. A sergeant took away my civilian clothes and made me stand in my underwear while he searched for a uniform. Since I was late, and the rest of the recruits had already been outfitted, there were hardly any uniforms left. He finally returned with a jacket whose sleeves didn't reach past my elbows, pants that fell just below my knees, and boots that were six sizes too small. The only thing that fit was the cap.

I was sent to my barracks. My fellow college recruits and I were told that the next morning the colonel and sergeant would arrive to review our troop. We were told to press our clothes and shine our shoes. Why should I shine my shoes when I can't even wear them, I thought. The only thing I did before going to bed was find a rope so I could tie my pants closed—buttoning them was out of the question.

The bugles sounded at 5:00 A.M. Our troop lined up quickly. I stood at the end of the line with my shoes in my hand and my pants tied with a rope. I also turned my cap sideways. I don't know how I got that stupid idea, but it seemed to go well with the rest of the outfit. The colonel entered our barracks and shouted for us to stand at attention. Then he addressed us. "If any of you don't follow orders for the next three months, if any of you do anything wrong," he shouted, "you will never see the light of day. We will throw you in jail forever." That was his wonderful greeting.

The colonel began to review our troop. "Shine your shoes, press your collar, stand up straight, look up, look down, look at me, don't look at me . . ." he barked. Then he reached me and his eyes bulged. When he finished screaming at me, he had me thrown in jail for failing to dress appropriately. As the military police dragged me out of the barracks, I tried to tell him that the uniform I had been given was too small, but he wouldn't listen. I worked in the jail for five days—cleaning toilets. On the fifth afternoon they sent me back to my barracks.

The next morning the bugles sounded at 5:00 A.M. and we lined up for review. Five minutes later I was back in jail. I had still not been given any clothes or boots that fit, yet the colonel had once again ordered me to prison because of my unacceptable appearance. When they finally released me, I was once again ordered back to my barracks. I'm not going back there, I thought, and I headed toward the general's office. I planned to talk to the colonel's superior and explain my situation. Unfortunately, I ran into the colonel on my way. He began to scream that I was a deserter. I was thrown into jail for twelve more days.

When I was finally released from jail I ran as fast as I could to the general's office. When the general saw me, he said, "What the hell happened to you, boy?" I told him that the first night I arrived I had been given clothes that didn't fit, and because I wasn't dressed well the colonel had thrown me in jail three times. "I've been cleaning toilets for a month. Should I just go back to the jail and plan on cleaning them until the end of my training?" I asked. The general wrote me a note to give the colonel if he tried to send me back to jail. Then he told me to return to my barracks.

The next morning the colonel once again screamed at me and ordered me back to jail. "No way," I yelled back. "I'm not going, I have a note from the general." The look that the colonel gave me could have killed. He couldn't send me to jail, but he could make my life outside of jail just as miserable as cleaning toilets, and he did.

Every day my troop went for an eight-mile run. We had to run with gas masks on, and two of the troop had to carry a large machine gun. The gun barrel was usually given to one soldier, and another soldier dragged the base of the gun, which was on wheels. The colonel ordered me to pull the whole damn thing—the gun and its base. It was incredibly heavy, and almost impossible for me to pull uphill because I had still not received boots and was wearing only my sandals. After a few miles I fell behind the others. To hell with this, I thought, and I ripped off my gas mask. I walked for the next hour, finally catching up with my troop as they were finishing learning army techniques for crawling under barbed wire. Just as I sat to rest, we were ordered to line up, put our gas masks on, and resume our run. The colonel ordered me to continue dragging the machine gun.

I ran for a few hundred yards; when the troop rounded the first bend I slowed to a walk. I just couldn't run with that damn machine gun. Then I got an idea. The rest of the run was downhill, and that sucker I was pulling was on wheels . . . I secured the gun to its base and climbed on board. The ride began slowly, but as the hill steepened I began to fly! The road was made of granite blocks, and as I rolled down the hill, me on top of the gun base with the gun barrel between my legs, that sucker made an unbelievable noise. I had the greatest time—*yahoo!* I was really flying, and figured I'd just keep riding until the ground became level.

It had been some time since I'd seen my troop, and I was sure that they were already back at the barracks. I had just rounded a curve at top speed and let out a thunderous *yeehaw*, when I spotted my fellow recruits. They were lined up on the side of the road, and the colonel was giving a speech. When the colonel turned and saw me riding atop the gun, straddling the barrel, and waving my cap in the air like a rodeo rider, he had a nervous breakdown—he tried to jump in front of me! I had no brakes or steering, and I'm still not sure how I managed to avoid hitting him. As I flew by, I knew I was in the deepest trouble of my life, I knew that the military was going to imprison me forever. So I decided not to stop. I figured if that was the situation, I might as well ride back to the barracks and get a few moments of relaxation before I was sent to jail.

I was sent back to jail. Two days after my latest incarceration began, the general I had spoken with about my lack of clothing came to the jail to inspect the inmates, and when he saw me he told the guards to release me. "I told you this fellow is to go free, it's not his fault that we didn't have the right clothes for him," he said. The general hadn't heard about my latest adventure, and I didn't provide him with details.

For the remainder of my service I made a concerted effort to stay out of trouble. I believe the general must have spoken to my colonel, because he stopped picking on me, which helped me in my efforts. I completed my military training and immediately left for Lupeni and Marta. Most important, when I left the army my spirit was intact.

5.

November 28, 1963

Marta and I were married on November 28, 1963. I walked in the pouring rain from Vulcan, and Marta walked in the pouring rain from Lupeni, to the mayor's office in between the two tiny towns. We had a brief ceremony—she said yes, I said yes, and we were declared husband and wife. We kissed each other and then walked back to our respective jobs to teach afternoon classes. We spent our honeymoon in a small apartment we had rented in Lupeni. We were unbelievably happy! We were in love, we were together, and we were both involved with towns that desperately needed us.

The village of Vulcan was small, rural, and poor. It had never had a physical education program. My elementary school kids had never played in organized games or had athletic contests. I rubbed my hands together and began to work. Each day I organized a different activity for the students—some days we had soccer games or volleyball tournaments, other days we had rugby matches. The school was turned upside down. It became an exciting institution in a village where nothing else was going on.

We had a great time until the weather turned bad. Winter hit hard. It was viciously cold, and I couldn't let the kids play outdoors—when they got wet, they had nothing to change into. In addition, their clothing was not warm enough for the weather, and I hated to see how they destroyed their little shoes in the snow. In Vulcan we had no gymnasium for the kids, and when I could no longer teach them outdoors, I had to find a way to create an indoor physical education area.

In those days the floors of our school were covered with a black oily liquid that protected them from damage. The liquid smelled miserable and I couldn't let the kids play on the floor and ruin their clothes. I started to ask townspeople if they had any old mattresses that we could put on the floor. Vulcan was a very poor mining town and the responses were all the same. "Bela, people don't even have enough mattresses for their own children to sleep on—no one has anything left over for their kids to play with, and no coal miner is going to care much about their child's physical education class."

Coal miners in Rumania led a very sad and difficult life. They spent most of their existence underground. Every morning they faced the fact that they might never get out of the mine alive. Accidents happened all the time. As soon as they got out they'd go to a beer joint and drink until they fell flat. Then the wife and the children would come to the bar with a wheelbarrow and cart their man home. In the process they would check his pockets for whatever remaining money he had.

Coal miners didn't know too much about their children. If you asked a miner how many kids he had, he'd tell you to ask his wife. I was not surprised that I got no response when I asked the miners for mattresses. I turned to one of my aunts, who was living in a small town near Vulcan. She was a teacher, continuing in her father's tradition, on the mountainside. I asked her if she could find some old mattresses. Within days she had several delivered to my school.

That is how I first began teaching indoors, and that's how I first began coaching gymnastics. It was a revolution for Vulcan. There had never before been any organized gymnastic activity in that town. On the first day of gymnastics practice I had the kids take off their pants and shirts so they wouldn't ruin their clothes. Those kids had only one pair of socks, pants, underwear, shirts, shoes, and so on. We had no gym clothes to give the kids, but they needed a certain freedom of movement for class, and I didn't want anyone to split their pants and get into trouble. The kids began practicing in their underwear.

"We are Catholic people and we have a fear of God. We don't want a pervert telling our children to take off their clothes!" The morning after our first gymnastics class the mothers of Vulcan came with their brooms and shovels, screaming that I was a pervert, an evil man, a corrupter of children. As I approached the mob, I listened to the principal of the school defend my actions. "Bela Karolyi isn't telling your children to be naked, he is just trying to protect their clothes while they do exercises. . . ." The women kept yelling that I was a pervert from a big town. It was time to step forward.

"Listen up, ladies," I began, "do you want your children to ruin their clothes?" They kept shouting that I was the enemy. "It is part of the school program that your children take physical education class," I continued. "Whether or not you like it, they have got to take my class. If you want them to destroy their clothes, fine, I'll send them home with their shirts and pants ripped." The crowd slowly moved away from the school, unsatisfied, but knowing that they could not fight the school system and did not have the money to buy their children new clothing.

There was always an anger and frustration against newcomers in primitive towns like Vulcan. Anybody who came from a bigger town, who was better dressed, or rode in a car, or tried to change the balance of their lives was immediately disliked. Their reaction to my efforts was spontaneous and understandable—one of the only things they had in life was the certainty of an elementary school for their children. A change in that school's format was like an earthquake to them.

Fortunately, it didn't take long for the mothers to calm down. Some old-timer in Vulcan remembered my grandfather, and pretty soon everyone knew that I wasn't a swell-headed young man from a big town who had come to disturb Vulcan and its children. I was accepted as a local; a man who had grown up in a town like theirs and had chosen to come home to give something back to the people.

When my gym students arrived the second afternoon of practice, I took off my shirt and pants and began to coach in my shorts and T-shirt. Slowly, one by one, the kids took off their shirts and pants and, in their underwear, joined in the class. I immediately set up reciprocal communications with the kids. I told them, "You respect me, and I'm going to respect you. If we do that, we are going to do great things together." I did not accept anyone fooling around, or not following the rules set up for their own safety.

We had the time of our lives. The kids and I became very close, and they followed me around like a god—they would have gone through fire for me. I demanded discipline, which they had never experienced before, and I gave them challenges and contests that made them feel like they were worth something.

I began to teach my kids about gymnastic preparation and tumbling. The kids were first through fourth graders, little guys, and they were dedicated customers. They showed up every afternoon, day after day, without fail. They were my first team, and together we made history in Vulcan.

At the end of the school year, Marta and I decided that we would hold an athletic spectacle, featuring a gymnastics show, for the towns of Vulcan and Lupeni. Marta made up a dance program for the gymnasts, and I worked on a tumbling program. We made two balance beams out of wood and boxes, and taught the kids how to do walkovers and cartwheels on them. They were the perfect body type for gymnastics, small and lean—coal miners' children were always on their feet and their diet didn't allow them to grow too much. It was amazing the natural abilities in excess of their body type that the kids exhibited.

The athletic show was the first time that I had offered anything for the whole town to see. No miner had ever gone to a musical show or an athletic show in his life. Shows cost money, and miners had nothing to spare. We held our free show on a Sunday afternoon and combined gymnastics with track and field and handball. We also offered hot dogs and beer that we paid for out of our meager school salaries. The entire community came.

The gymnastics exhibition was the finale of the athletic show. The crowd was silent as we pulled out our mattresses and homemade balance beams. When the kids began their dances and their tumbling routines the crowd began to clap and cheer—they had never seen anything like it. By the end of the show old people were crying, and the mothers who had threatened me with their brooms were hugging and kissing me. I had given them something to be proud of—and I had given their children pride in themselves.

Miners are not the type of people who walk up to you and thank you, but these people did. They came up to me with tears in their eyes. "I never even knew how many children I had," one miner told me. "I appreciate the work you've done . . . I'm so proud of my children." It was something to see them hugging their little ones, some for the first time in their lives.

That afternoon people told me stories about my grandfather. That meant so much to me, because in my family we weren't really allowed to talk about him once he had left. He wasn't someone my grandmother was proud of, but the people of Vulcan had loved him.

That day was a turning point in my life. My choice of occupation, my beliefs, my goals, all seemed very right. I was the happiest person in the world. I felt important, satisfied, and appreciated by the people.

The next year the first high school opened in Vulcan, and we were able to have Marta transferred to my school. Together we created the biggest athletic activity center that the Jiul Valley (the valley where the mining communities in Rumania were located) had ever seen. Children from all the surrounding towns came to Vulcan to attend high school. They were pretty wild kids—children with little education who had been undisciplined since their elementary years. It was frightening to stand in front of them and direct them. But I did. I gave them discipline and challenges and they responded.

Vulcan became like a volcano—boiling with activity. Now that I had high school kids to work with we had the power necessary to face other high school teams in track and field and team handball. We began to travel for competitions. We beat everybody. It was unbelievable, the physical and mental dedication of our kids was 200 percent compared to the usual 75 percent that other kids put into their sports.

Part of the reason my kids excelled was that they were frustrated and angry. I'm a poor kid, they all thought, but I can show that I'm worthy, dammit, it doesn't matter where I came from, I can win. With my coaching and my support, I fed their appetites for success. We rolled through the National Championships in handball and track and field, and competed against teams from big-time clubs. We were beaten from time to time, but we never left the arena without giving our best.

The miners did all the fund-raising for our trips. They were so proud of their kids—they lived through their children's accomplishments. Eventually they raised enough money for gymnastics equipment and we created our first real gymnasium. That's when we really began to train and prepare our gymnasts to compete at the national level.

I will never forget our first National Gymnastic Championship. It was in Bucharest, the Rumanian capital, and my little kids had been working for two and a half years for that one competition. They had traveled a bit, but they had never been out of the Jiul Valley, let alone to the big city of Bucharest. The kids were seven to eleven years of age—the traditional gymnasts of the time were in their mid-twenties with some still competing in their thirties.

When we entered the arena we saw all the big clubs that had been funded by the government or by industry. There was the army's club, the Dinamo (the secret police) club, all the factory and mill clubs. We were from a tiny mining town, with no money or government support, and my kids were half the size and more than half the age of the other competitors.

"Look at the itty-bitty babies, they're so cute," the gymnasts and coaches said as they petted my kids. Then they asked me if we were there to watch the competition. "We are not here to watch," I answered, "we are here to compete." They laughed, and then the objections flew. They said that our being there was an insult to the national champion and so on and so on. Finally, because our team had qualified as regional winners, we were given the green light.

After the compulsories we were not close to the first three teams. However, by the time the optionals ended we were among the first six teams in the nation. Our optional programs had been daring, unique displays of tiny talents. No one had ever seen some of the gymnastics performed by our kids. No one had ever imagined that gymnasts as young as ours had such fantastic power and talent. As a result, we created a very obvious conflict. Everything up until that moment which had been called gymnastics came into question. The ages of my kids, their power and style, all made the big teams look bad. The Gymnastics Federation decided to eliminate the conflict by eliminating our chance to compete in the Nationals for the next several years. It was a simple process. The Federation set an age limit of fourteen for National competitors that we could not possibly meet. We were out.

For the next four years my kids won all the local and regional competitions. They were not, however, allowed to compete in the Senior National Competitions because of the age limit. Finally, in 1967, after four years of protests by our local mining community leaders, the Federation allowed my team to compete.

The miners, some of whom had never been out of their villages since they were born, organized a train convoy to the 1967 National Championships. They were going to support their kids no matter how far they had to travel. They invaded the town where the Nationals were held, and there were quite a few conflicts in the local drinking establishments. The competition itself was like the wildest football or soccer game you've ever seen—cheering from the first to the last moment, one hand holding a glass of beer, the other clenched in a fist.

Most important was the competition. It was like nothing anyone in Rumania, or the world, had ever seen before. My kids' performances were based on a new type of gymnastics—physical gymnastics. I had taken my knowledge of athletics and transferred everything I knew into gymnastics. I knew that the stronger my kids were, the better athletes they would be. I also knew that the stronger they were physically, the stronger they'd be mentally. We had spent a tremendous amount of time lifting weights, running, jumping, rope climbing—everything I learned in track and field I reintroduced into gymnastics.

That was how I created the dynamic, powerful, aggressive type of performer first seen in 1968. Gymnasts who did not just give technical performances but physically impressive performances. The height of their somersaults, the difficulty levels of their tumbling passes, were all raised. I hadn't perfected my system yet, but I had shown my country that a new type of gymnast and a new level of ability was on the horizon.

We had the most successful competition we had ever had. The train ride home was quite a celebration. The miners had decorated the train for the kids with posters and flags. It was an unbelievable ride, so much joy. For the following five days the entire Jiul Valley celebrated the accomplishment of the children.

For every action there is a reaction—that is something I have learned time and again throughout my life as a coach. The reaction from our local community was fantastic. It was less so from the central authorities. The Education Ministry accused me of local patriotism and a twisting of the Communist directives. The Gymnastics Federation, composed of egomaniacs and politicians who cared only for their own careers, accused me of overemphasizing the importance of sports activities in the school. Why? They were angered by my popularity in the Jiul Valley and by the results of my efforts at the Nationals. All sorts of negative regulations were passed.

The miners in Rumania were one of the most powerful social forces in the country. They were aggressive men, and if they were angered beyond reason a civil war could erupt. They heard about the regulations that the Ministry was placing on their schools' sports activities, and they marched to the Ministry to demand justice for their children. For a time the negative regulations were dropped. But even then, at the start of my career, I learned that the Ministry and the Federation had an agenda that was quite different from mine. Both organizations were filled with men who cared more for their paychecks and their careers than they did for the glory of their country and its children. From that point forward they began watching me like hawks. I knew they would silently wait for me to make a mistake, and when I did, they would swoop down for the kill.

Our gymnastic program continued to evolve. The gymnastics we were doing was no longer the sport that Marta and I had learned in college. It was a new type of sport, based on maximum physical fitness and preparation. We practiced ten times more than any other team, and we were getting ten times better. The following year we swept most of the competitions. Our accomplishment did not go unnoticed.

I was contacted by the Education Ministry. "Bela, how would you like to be a part of the first experimental gymnastics school in the country?" the Ministry people asked. I was told that the school needed ambitious young coaches, and that the Ministry would provide money for all of the teachers and coaches as well as for excellent equipment and facilities. It was a big project, something I had never dreamed could be done. I was thrilled to be involved. I thought the Ministry had recognized our efforts as coaches and the accomplishments of our gymnasts. I accepted the position and we moved to Onesti.*

I would not realize until much later that most everything done by Rumanian organizations was done to win favor with the government. That type of favor meant more money, and more opportunities for the officials involved. For the Ministry, a gymnastics school that produced champions would also yield government favor. I was simply a means to this end.

---

* In 1975, ten years after I left Vulcan, I received a letter from the village inviting me to the ten-year anniversary of the first high school graduation. I went, and learned that twenty-one of my first twenty-seven students had become physical education teachers.

6.

Creating a Gymnastics Program

Creating an experimental gymnastics school in Onesti was a dream we had never dared hope for. It was also one of the most difficult projects we had ever undertaken. Marta and I had our hands full. We had taken our team from the Jiul Valley to the new school in Onesti, and we were trying to provide housing, meals, and instruction for the kids in addition to finding new gymnasts. We also had administrative responsibilities. I had never been involved with administration before, and I quickly found out I enjoyed instruction much more than organization.

We tested about four thousand children. I went from elementary school to elementary school testing for speed, flexibility, coordination, and balance. I set up mats in each classroom and taught the kids somersaults, headstands, and backbends. I also organized races and balancing contests. It was fairly easy to see who had flexibility and coordination, even in the youngest children. By the fourth week of testing, we still hadn't found enough kids for the school.

And I wasn't satisfied with the physical quality and the natural talent of the children we had found. I decided to screen for gymnasts one more time.

Recreation period is a great time to watch kids without getting directly involved in their activities, and I spent hour after hour watching kids play. Racing games, climbing games, jumping games—the children I observed were active, but they weren't gymnasts. Then one day I saw two little blond-headed girls doing cartwheels in the corner of the school yard. I approached and watched them very closely—they had something. *Brrrrring!* The school bell rang and the little ones darted inside.

Where did they disappear to? I went from class to class, but I did not recognize the girls' faces. All I had seen were skinny legs and blonde ponytails. "Who likes gymnastics?" I'd ask the kids in each classroom I visited. They didn't even know what the word *gymnastics* meant. "Okay," I tried, "gymnastics is a sport where you do cartwheels. Who can do a cartwheel?" The kids would raise their hands and I'd have them do their cartwheels for me. "Very nice," I'd say, but they weren't the ones.

I was ready to give up. It was the end of the day and I had been to every class. I stopped for one last try. "Can anyone do a cartwheel?" I tiredly asked. No answer. I was ready to walk out when I saw two little blonde heads in the back of the room. "Hey," I called, "can either of you do cartwheels?" They whispered to each other and then nodded yes. "Let me see them," I said. *Boom, boom*—they did perfect cartwheels.

"You guys are the ones doing cartwheels in the corner of the school yard," I said. They nodded. "What are your names?" I asked them. "Viorica Dumitru" and "Nadia Comaneci," they answered. I told them to tell their mothers that Bela Karolyi said they could be admitted to Onesti's experimental gymnastics school if they wished. They were six years old at the time.

I placed Nadia and Viorica, and all of the little ones, in the same pattern of preparation that I had begun to use in Vulcan. Intensive physical preparation, work with weights and ropes, and lots of running and jumping in addition to their gymnastic training. After three months we held our first contest to see how the little ones were progressing and to give them a fun day—they received gifts and trophies for their efforts. The big star of the day, the one that popped like a big star among her group, was Viorica, not Nadia.

Nadia Comaneci was a very quiet child. She hardly smiled during those first few months at Onesti, and she didn't stand out in her group. She did, however, have one trait that eventually caught my attention. She never said "no," or "I cannot do that." It didn't matter what the stunt was, how difficult or frightening, she was always ready to perform. That enabled her to progress very rapidly, and in a short time she could do the same feats as the older gymnasts at the school. Nadia, however, was still very young, and her skills did not eliminate the possibility of mistakes or falls. In fact, when we took the kids to their first Junior National Championship, about a year after she'd joined our school, Nadia fell off the beam three times. She'd fall, get excited as she tried to get back on, and then fall off the other side. That was how Nadia began her gymnastics career.

Nadia never had the opportunity to develop an attitude or become spoiled, because she was always surrounded by other talented gymnasts. Gymnasts in our school who were the same age as Nadia had similar capabilities and potential.

In 1972, after four years of preparation and practice, Nadia's generation was ready for its first international competition—the Friendship Cup in Bulgaria. Marta and I did not have a lot of international competitive gymnastics experience. Marta had been a good college gymnastics competitor, but she had not competed internationally. We weren't sure how good the other teams would be. We didn't know that the Soviets were considered unbeatable. We had no idea that the Germans and Czechs consistently placed second and third to the Russians. We were from a small and isolated country.

Everyone on our team was approximately ten years old. The gymnasts from the other countries were in their late teens and twenties. They were graceful queens like Ukrainian Ludmila Turi-scheva, beautiful moving gymnasts with nothing to say. They were the ideal of everything that gymnastics could offer—up until the point when my kids performed in the Friendship Cup.

The little guys versus the big guys. It was just like our first National Championships in Rumania with the kids from Vulcan. My kids were exploding bombs, dynamos who twisted, turned, and flipped without any kind of concern for failure. My kids had no fears. Their tremendous physical preparation gave them the oppor-tunity to perform superior gymnastic tricks and performances—it was totally shocking for the other teams.

Nadia won the all-around gold, and the team won the silver medal. Most remarkable, we beat all the famous international gym-nasts, the glory of the Soviet Union and Germany. A new type of gymnastics had been placed on the floor, and the past leaders did not have the formula to bring themselves up to our level. The Friendship Cup was a warning sign for them. They had to change with the times or prepare to lose to Rumania.

The Russians considered our performance a fluke. The Germans, who have always been a more studious and scientific people, began to bribe our government officials for the chance to watch me coach and my gymnasts train. We had a lot of fun at their expense. The Germans would bring video cameras into our gymnasium and tape our practices. I would call the kids over to one corner and they would huddle around me while I whispered jokes in their ears. The Germans thought this was some special ritual—we were just talking nonsense. In later competitions I saw the Germans performing our "secret ritual" with their kids. It was comical.

In the meantime, the Soviets, who are not studious like the

Germans but instead practical, came to realize the value of our preparation, and they began to train their gymnasts in the same way I trained Rumania's team. The Communist system was so well integrated in those days that all the material the Germans produced was translated for the Russians. The Russians swept away their old system. Based on the sheer numbers of participants they could generate in comparison with a country as small as Rumania, ten thousand to our eight gymnasts, they caught up to our level of gymnastics relatively quickly.

Well, they almost caught up. I have a theory about copying, just as I have a theory about the winner always being the one who puts in the most hours of preparation. I have never copied anyone—in the old days there was no one for me to copy, since I had not seen any Russian or German gymnasts perform prior to the Friendship Cup. But if I had copied them, that meant that I would have been almost as good as them in the competition. Almost as good, but never quite as good. I would never in my life catch up to the one I copied, because they would always be a hair's breadth or two ahead of me. As long as I based my efforts on catching someone else, I would always be behind. The Germans and the Russians could copy us, but they couldn't catch us.

The Germans and the Russians were not our biggest concern in the early 1970s. We had plenty of enemies in our own backyard. The other clubs in Rumania had watched our rise in the gymnastics community, and they were hell-bent on trying to destroy our growing strength. Our fiercest enemy was Dinamo, the secret police club in Rumania. They had political power and money, and that meant that you could be history if you crossed them. Dinamo had a gymnastics club that had unbelievable financial support and capabilities. Until my team came on the scene, Dinamo's club dominated gymnastics in Rumania. Their members were always chosen for the big international competitions as well as for the Olympic Games.

In an effort to destroy the strength of our team, Dinamo began to bribe the parents of many of my gymnasts. "Here is a home, a car, money to pay off your debts . . . just switch your child's gymnastic club," they would tell parents. They recruited gymnasts from my own team! As a result, Dinamo's team was always a realistic power. However, they could never beat us, even with our gymnasts, because once they stole the kids they didn't know how to train them.

The Rumanian Gymnastics Federation worked hand in hand with Dinamo. The members of the Federation enjoyed living the good life, and Dinamo provided the money and political power that allowed them to live so well. It was therefore no surprise when, in 1975, the Federation announced that three of Dinamo's gymnasts would comprise Rumania's team for the European Championship in Norway. None of my gymnasts were chosen, even though their performances in past competitions had been superior to those of Dinamo's gymnasts.

The 1975 European Championship in Norway was an important international competition. Only one year before the Olympics, it was a chance for gymnasts to make an international name for themselves. Each country was allowed to present three competitors—two to compete and two alternates, or three to compete and one alternate—in whatever combination they chose. Rumania had chosen to present two competitors and one alternate. I saw an opportunity to force the Federation to open a position for one more alternate. I saw a chance to get one of my kids into the championship.

The Ministry of Education was still supporting our school in Onesti and my position as head coach of that institution. After the Friendship Cup, they were extremely receptive to my requests because our success had made them look good in the eyes of the government. Since the Ministry was a political power in Rumania, I turned to them for help in getting the Gymnastics Federation to open another position on the European Championship team. It was in the Ministry's best interests to find a way to open another position. Together, we successfully fought for another designated alternate position.

On the train ride home to Onesti from the Ministry's office in Bucharest I thought about which gymnast from my team I would choose to go to the Championship. A sweet little gymnast named Teadora Ungureanu (Dorina) was one of the best in my club, and I thought she might be the one to go. There were, however, others with great abilities, and of course Nadia was getting better and better every day.

"All right," I said to the kids the next morning. "We have the chance to take one of you to the European Championship in Norway." The kids cheered. "We are going to have a competition tomorrow afternoon, and the gymnast who performs the best will go to Norway," I explained. Everybody was excited—they all wanted that chance. Everybody except Dorina.

"Dorina," I said, "what's the matter?" Dorina was a cute girl, a tiny brunette, full of energy. On that day her face was very pale and her eyes were red. "What's wrong, Dorina?" I asked. "Nothing, sir," she said. "Good, then go for it, you'll do great in tomorrow's competition." I was pretty sure that Dorina would be the one chosen to go to Norway. However, halfway through the workout, I walked over to her and rested my hand on her head—she was burning up! "Dorina, you've got a fever, do you feel bad?" "Yes," she answered, and coughed a bit. "I think I have a cold," she said. "Okay, you go home and take some aspirin. We'll see you tomorrow."

The next morning Dorina came into the gym with her mother. Her little eyes were puffy and red and her face was burning up. She insisted on performing, but her performance just wasn't convincing. The one who grew wings was Nadia. It was then that Nadia's true personality surfaced. She was a fighter, the one who could find the weakness of her competitor. If her competitor fell off the beam or messed up her floor routine, Nadia grew wings and swooped in on her opponent. On that day she was visibly superior to the rest of the team.

Deep in my heart I felt so sorry for Dorina. Marta and I still considered sending her to the Championship, but we didn't know if she would be better by then. "Bela, if you bring Dorina and she does not do well everybody at the Ministry is going to blame us. We will never be able to justify why we sent a sick gymnast," Marta said. She was right. Six days later Nadia and I headed to Norway.

The Federation and Dinamo had decided that two Rumanian gymnasts would compete and one would be an alternate in the European Championship. Anka Grigoras and Alina Goreac, two of Dinamo's gymnasts, were set to compete. The coach from Dinamo had no interest in having a third competitor, even though we had that option. That was such a waste—it decreased our chances to win the competition and it robbed one of our gymnasts of important international competition experience. I wanted my kid to have that experience and exposure. Dammit, I thought, I'm going to go over to the organizers and see if I can have Nadia designated as Rumania's third performer. I did not inform the coach from Dinamo what I was doing—the hell with him, I thought.

"I want the Rumanian team to have three gymnasts competing," I told the organizers of the Championship. They said that wasn't possible because we had already signed up to have two gymnasts compete and one be the alternate. "Well," I said, "that was a damn mistake." They told me too bad. I made a huge scene, "Dammit, dammit," I yelled, and pounded on the table. I looked over at the Germans, they were lining up four gymnasts to compete—not three gymnasts and an alternate. I jumped to the skies and screamed at the injustice.

The organizers had made a mistake and allowed the German team to have four gymnasts compete. They had forgotten to make one of the gymnasts an alternate. "Goddamn those Germans, they are getting favoritism," I yelled. That's when a dark-haired woman who was standing behind me began to scream and argue with me. Her name was Ellen Berger, and she was the coach of the East German team.

The organizers became concerned. Ellen Berger and I were creating an international confrontation (it would not be our last). They decided that since they had made a mistake with the German team, they'd allow Rumania to have one more gymnast compete. I wrote down Nadia's name on the official form. Nadia was in.

At the 1975 European Championship, Ludmila Turischeva was the Olympic and World Champion. Turischeva was a statuesque gymnast, very beautiful to watch, trained in the old style of gymnastics. She was considered unbeatable. Nadia beat the hell out of her. My little gymnast twisted, flipped, and turned without missing a beat. Nadia tore through the competition, and in the end, she had won four gold medals, including the all-around European Champion title.

It was the end of an era. Turischeva, the queen of gymnastics, had been dethroned. She walked up to Nadia, just a little itty-bitty kid, and congratulated her. She never complained, she just congratulated Nadia and then walked away with a sad look, a look of resignation.

Nadia had gotten the chance to become the European Champion purely by luck. If I had not gotten one of my gymnasts designated as an alternate, if Dorina had not gotten sick, if I had not fought to get Nadia named as a competitor, Nadia would not have had the opportunity to compete in the Championship. She took her opportunity and she made it golden. From that moment on nobody could beat her.

The Education Ministry was thrilled. They were in direct competition with the Gymnastics Federation, both being government organizations with competing interests in gymnastics. The Federation and Ministry were always fighting to see who was the strongest, and who could gain the most favor with the government. The Ministry had finally won a round. As for me, I was proud of Nadia, and happy. I wasn't too worried about angering the Federation, as long as the Ministry continued to support my school. The Federation didn't pay me, so I didn't feel obligated to respond to them. Later I would realize that this attitude was a mistake. Regardless of whether or not they paid my salary, the Federation controlled most of Rumania's gymnastics programs, and that meant they ultimately controlled me.

The Rumanian Gymnastics Federation enjoyed Nadia's victory; however, they were disturbed by the rise of a gymnast from a gymnastics school they did not directly control. They were also not happy that Nadia was being coached by the Karolyis—because of our disagreements in the past. The Dinamo club, too, was angered at the rise of one of our gymnasts, and at the fact that I had not informed Dinamo's coach at the European Championship of my intentions. I had created a conflict with two of the most powerful organizations in Rumania. They would ultimately destroy me.

7.

1976

The Olympic Games were one of the most important reasons that Rumania pumped money into sports. Olympic visibility was used as a political propaganda tool. Our athletes represented the power of our government system and way of life—that's truly how our government thought.

In 1976, every gymnastics club in Rumania wanted to provide an athlete for the country's Olympic team. Big athletes generated more money and privileges for clubs and coaches. By 1976, I had been named the coach of the experimental gymnastic school in Onesti. After Nadia became the European Champion the Ministry was in seventh heaven. They were receiving a lot of attention from the government, and the school in Onesti was flooded with important visitors. I was given a free hand to run the gymnastics program and to designate which gymnasts would compete in national competitions.

In June 1976, we traveled to the Rumanian National Championship. We ended up with the first six places, the team gold medal, and a sense of satisfaction. My kids were the best in Rumania, and in the Olympics they might prove to be the best gymnasts in the world. Nadia had truly come into her own. She was mentally and physically powerful—unbeatable. It never entered my mind that my team would not be the Rumanian Olympic team. We had won the Nationals, while Dinamo's club had only placed two gymnasts on the national team. The top six gymnasts on the national team were to become the Olympic team—those were my kids.

Three days after the Nationals I received an official Olympic entry form from the Rumanian Gymnastics Federation. The form listed our country's Olympic gymnastic team—four gymnasts from Dinamo and three of my students from Onesti, one of whom was Nadia. How in the world? My kids had earned their places! I immediately called the Federation. I spoke with one of the many Federation officials and demanded that Dinamo's gymnasts be replaced by my own. "If you want to cut your own neck be my guest," the official said to me. "Run into the wall if you want, but I won't commit suicide, I won't oppose Dinamo. . . . I have a good position here."

No one in the Federation was willing to stand up to Dinamo. They were all afraid of losing their jobs and their financial security. I had nothing to lose. I went to Bucharest, to the Communist party building, to try to speak with the government official responsible for the 1976 Olympic Games. I stood for almost six hours until I was finally allowed to face the fellow in charge. I explained the problem. "We have won the right to compete, as a team, in the Olympics," I began. "Nadia Comaneci is the European Champion, the rest of the team has beaten every other gymnast in our country. We won the Nationals, and historically that means we should be the chosen team."

The man was a coward. He was afraid to make a decision on his own. His cowardice, however, worked in my favor. He decided that there would be a final selection of the Olympic team based on a competition to be held in Bucharest. "We already had that competition, it was called the National Championship," I said in frustration. "If you want more of your gymnasts on the Olympic team then come to Bucharest and face the final test," he spat. "Well, I really want more people, so I'll be there," I said and left his office.

We moved the team to Bucharest. It was a hot summer, hot, hot, hot, and the kids really suffered from the heat. They were in a new gym, with new equipment, surrounded by athletes training for different sports at the center. It was very difficult to keep the kids focused on the important thing, the preparation. We had three weeks before the final test.

The gymnastics team from Dinamo was also training at the center in Bucharest. We were given a set schedule that both teams were to follow. Two training times, morning and afternoon, were scheduled. Dinamo's team, however, rarely showed up for the morning workout, and many times skipped the afternoon session. My team never missed a practice, not even the ones scheduled for Saturday and Sunday. We usually had the entire gymnasium to ourselves.

One Sunday morning, about a week before the final competition, I was on the floor and Marta was by the beam working with the girls. We heard voices and turned to see eight or ten people walk into the gymnasium. One of those people was the general in charge of all sports in Rumania. He was the biggest big shot in Rumanian sports. There were also several people from the Federation, and they were crowded around a short man I didn't know.

I stopped our workout. The rule was that whenever anyone in a superior position came into a room we had to give them a report. I lined up the kids. "Comrade General," I began, "these are some of the gymnasts training for a final competition to decide whether they will be part of the Olympic team. My team is preparing for the 1976 Olympic Games and we are working on our floor routines and our compulsory beam routines. I ask your permission to continue our workout." He thanked me and then turned and saluted the short man standing in the middle of the official group. Holy cow, I thought, that man must be a real big shot if the general has to report to him.

"Comrade Secretary of Propaganda," the general began, and then related what I had told him. "I heard what Bela said," the party secretary said; "what I want to know is where are the rest of the gymnasts training to be part of the Olympic team?" The general was flustered and turned to me. "I have no idea where Dinamo's team is," I answered. The general told the party secretary that he would find Dinamo's coaches and gymnasts and he ran out of the room. I stood before the party secretary and waited. "Bela, everything is all right, go back to your workout," he said.

Fifteen minutes later a very red-faced general returned to the gymnasium. The party secretary asked where Dinamo's team was, and the general replied, "I have to report that they went to the beach." The party secretary stayed and watched my gymnasts for half an hour. Before he left, he called me over. "Bela, do you know who I am?" I didn't want to give the wrong answer and insult him— "Don't trouble yourself, Bela, I will tell you. My name is Ilie Verdet, and I am originally from the mining area where your grandfather lived." I had never followed political careers, but I had heard that a man who had come from a miner's family had worked his way up the political ladder and become the Party Secretary of Propaganda. "Your grandfather was a great man," he told me. "I hope you do just as good a job."

Verdet scheduled a meeting for both my team and Dinamo's the following morning. We were told to be at the gym by 10:00 A.M. The next day the atmosphere was tense. Dinamo's coaches were running around like rats, the general was cussing at them because they had made him look bad in front of Verdet. Marta and I sat quietly in the corner.

The meeting began. "Are you the coach of the Dinamo team?"

Verdet asked one of the coaches. "Yes, Comrade," he answered. "Where was your team yesterday?" "Well, I could see that the girls were tired, so we took them out for recreational activity," the coach said. Verdet raised his voice, "You call a beach party an active recreational activity? Who did you report to that you would be taking the gymnasts to the beach?" "I'm not reporting to anyone, I'm the head coach," he answered. "You were the head coach," Verdet replied softly, "but you are not anymore. From now on Bela Karolyi is the person responsible for the National and Olympic team."

"Bela," said Verdet as he walked out of the room, "please report to me a week from now to tell me the names of the members of the Olympic team." That was it. I was in charge of the coaching, the schedule, and the selection. I wanted to be fair about the selection process—my ultimate goal was to make the Rumanian Olympic team the best team possible. I spent the next week watching all the gymnasts practice—both my kids and Dinamo's. The discrepancy between the two teams was so obvious and brutal that I knew that I just couldn't make a winning team if I took 50 percent of the team from Dinamo's kids. In the end, I took six from my club and two alternates from Dinamo to the 1976 Olympics in Montreal, Canada.

From that moment on some of the members of Dinamo and the Federation no longer just disliked me, they prepared to hunt me down.

8.

Survival

"**N**ow entering the arena for the 1976 Olympics, the team from Rumania!" No applause. The Soviets had been announced before us, and from the locker rooms we had heard wild clapping and cheers. A man ran up to me and yelled, "It's your turn, you must enter the arena." Once again the announcer boomed, "Now entering the arena, the Rumanian team!" The organizers of the 1976 Olympics ran around my team like crazy, desperately trying to push us toward the tunnel that led to the floor where the podium workout was being held. I pretended that I didn't understand what they wanted. We did not move.

Nobody in the West knew us in 1976. We went to the Olympic Games in Montreal as a little-known team from a small and relatively unheard of country. The Soviets were the reigning gymnastic champions—Ludmila Turischeva, and her teammate, Olga Korbut (already twenty-one years old), were the big names. Nadia Comaneci was just a tiny fourteen-year-old, 80 pounds of power and pigtails ready to burst upon the international scene.

There was a feeling of Soviet domination the moment we arrived in Montreal. Everyone was watching them. It was justified, and it didn't bother us. We had the quiet we needed to concentrate on the competition, and to adjust to the new time zone and equipment. And the kids had the chance to explore the Olympic Village. Back then the big thing was to exchange pins with athletes from around the world. The kids became expert pin changers.

The day of the podium workout finally arrived. This is the opportunity for gymnasts to practice, in a competitive format, on the floor where the competition will be held. They are not actually competing, but are given, as a team, fifteen minutes to work each apparatus. Usually, gymnasts play it safe—performing watered-down routines to avoid last-minute injuries. The public is allowed to watch these practices, and on the day of the podium workout for the 1976 Olympics the arena was full.

The audience and the media that watches the podium workout is an educated one. They are there because they are true fans of the sport, and they take the practice as a preview of things to come. At the 1976 Olympics podium workout, they focused on the Soviet team—the reigning Olympic champions and favorites in the East and the West.

No one knew who the Rumanian team was, but I knew that had to change. I knew that the focus had to be turned toward my kids. If the audience didn't show their appreciation for my team during the competition, if they didn't watch us as intently as they watched the Soviets, then the judges would not take us seriously either. There is a direct relationship between audience support and high scores, just as the most well-known gymnasts tend to be scored higher than the unknowns. I needed the audience and the media to make my team well known.

"Now entering the arena . . . *the Rumanian team!*" We still stood in the locker room, but the focus of the audience had changed. They were now paying attention to the double doorways through which our team was supposed to have entered the arena. I could hear the rumbling and the questions. The organizers were frantic. "Sir," Nadia whispered, "they are calling us to the floor, shouldn't we go in?" "Let them wait for us," I said. "Let us get the audience's attention."

I looked at my team. For the competition I had chosen snow-white leotards with thin red piping down the sides. I had all of the kids put their hair in pigtails, tied neatly with enormous red and white bows. They looked like tiny dolls. No junky T-shirts, no messy jackets or backpacks. I turned to my kids. "You all know what to do," I began. "Remember what we practiced, and make yourselves and your country proud. . . . The time has come, let's go get 'em!"

They marched into the arena like soldiers, *bac, bac, bac*, no head turned left or right. The kids went directly to the beam and lined up. "Nobody sit down," I cautioned. The size and cuteness of the kids, in sharp contrast to the rest of the competitors, had caught the public's and the media's attention, but we had just begun. One after another the kids performed their full competition routines on the beam. No watered-down versions, no sloppy mistakes. The crowd went crazy. By the time we reached the sixth person, Nadia, there wasn't a spectator, a photographer, or a reporter that wasn't watching. The camera flashes were going like fire. Nadia marched to the beam and performed a routine with a complexity and level of difficulty that had never before been seen. She stuck her dismount like glue.

Pure pandemonium! A few moments before the only team in the arena had been the Soviets; now we were the center of attention. We moved to the bars as the Russians began to practice their floor routines. Three or four of their gymnasts practiced at one time— very sloppy—while the rest sat. We still did not sit down. *Bang!*

One after another the kids executed their bar routines. My kids had powerful routines—they were so tiny that they had to fly between the bars to reach them! The people went nuts.

We continued the workout in the same way, *bac, bac, bac,* to each piece of equipment. By the end of the podium workout no one was even watching the Russians. It was one of the biggest strategic successes I have ever had. To turn the media and the public's attention so drastically was incredible. The next day we had to hide from reporters! I kept the kids away from public workouts—anything that would indicate what we were going to be doing in the competition. I wanted to keep a little bit of mystery about our team.

"Now entering the arena for the 1976 Olympic Games, *the Rumanian team!*" The applause was thunderous as we entered the arena for the compulsory portion of the Olympics—it was the greatest applause given to any team. Everything was center stage except the judging. There was still a strong traditional Soviet setup. Russian-affiliated judges dominated the judging scene because most of the judges came from Socialist countries and they played toward the Russian side. Their favoritism, however, wasn't too noticeable, and even favoritism couldn't have affected Nadia's scores—she was on fire.

My kids dominated the compulsories. By the time we reached our last event, the bars, we were only hundredths of a point behind the first-place team, the Russians. That's when Nadia stepped up to the bars and changed history. She flew between the bars, literally sailed through the air, with a flare and extension that had never before been seen. When she executed her dismount she landed like a stone. All hell broke loose in that arena.

Nadia and I walked to the bleachers to await her score. Moments later a 1.00 was flashed across the scoreboard. A 1.00, what's that mean? No one knew how to react. The crowd was silent, confused. I walked over to the judges. "Excuse me," I said, "it is very important for me to know what is Nadia's score?" That's when a Swedish judge, a very excited judge, held up ten fingers. "Ten? What is a ten? I want Nadia's score," I said. An announcer came on the loudspeaker.

"Ladies and Gentlemen, for the very first time in Olympic history, Nadia Comaneci has received the score of a perfect ten!" The organizers had not been prepared to score anyone with a perfect ten, they didn't have the numbers necessary for a 10 on the scoreboard. That's why they put up a 1.00. A perfect 10 . . . Golleee! The arena went crazy with celebration. I don't think there were more than fifteen Rumanians in the audience, but everyone celebrated the victory of a little girl who had come to Montreal and performed in an unprecedented manner.

Nadia never did show much emotion. She was a solitary person, separate from the other kids on the team. But on that day I could see a little smile in her eyes. She turned toward me and said, "Sir, is that really a ten?" "You bet it is, Nadia," I answered. "Oh, my God," she whispered.

Nadia received five more tens during the 1976 Olympics—three on the uneven bars, two on the beam. In the end, she won the Olympic all-around gold medal and became a part of history and a fixture in the future of gymnastics.

Of course there is a backlash to forcing the hand of the media and the public. Following the Olympics the sensation that we created threatened to overwhelm us. Immediately after the Games I asked to go home. There was no charter flight to Rumania, so we made a trip to a youth camp in Canada where the kids could relax and we could all avoid the media. Everybody wanted a part of Nadia and the rest of the team. It was frightening, and I was happy when we boarded a plane to return to Rumania.

Unreal; stepping off the plane in Bucharest was just unreal. We knew that the Rumanians were proud of us, but the turnout was overwhelming. President Nicolae Ceauşescu had received so many congratulatory calls that he went crazy and ordered our arrival to be a great celebration. Even Ceauşescu's wife, a woman who was extremely jealous of anyone who presented any competition to her or showed any special abilities in science, art, sports (whatever), was part of the celebration. The kids were too young to be a threat to her.

We returned to Onesti to restore normalcy to our lives and to the kids'. That was a pipe dream. Every five minutes the door to the gym opened and another delegation from this or that country marched through. They were accompanied by big shots from our government and the Gymnastics Federation. I had to stop practice, line the kids up, and present them to every delegation. It drove me completely crazy. The visitors, reporters, media were nonstop.

The kids' families went crazy. They were normal, average people living basic lives who were suddenly celebrities. They dragged their children all over, to grand openings, special events, and so on. They just lost their minds. The kids, too, went nuts. Under these conditions it was extremely difficult to provide a sturdy and consistent preparation. But we had to. Ceauşescu had invited us all to Bucharest for an awards ceremony and celebration. He planned to personally give out Rumanian government Orders (awards) to the kids and to Marta and me. He demanded that the team perform before the country at the ceremony.

We went to the awards ceremony in Bucharest. The kids were given monetary awards. I received the highest award that anyone involved with sports or the arts could receive—the First Grade Order of Labor. Marta also received an Order of Labor, as did Nicolae Vieru, the director of the Gymnastics Federation, and Geza Pozsar, our choreographer. However, Nicolae's award was a lesser grade than Marta's.

In a Socialist country, how you are positioned politically is very important—what your status with the government is and what recognition they grant to you. Our Orders granted privileges. We got a tax break, traveled for free on common transportation, and received monetary awards. Suddenly I was, for the first time in my life, politically set. I did not abuse my new privileges save one: my new access to hunting territories. I grew up hunting, I love to hunt, and the opportunity to hunt on land to which hardly anyone except the highest government officials had access was fantastic.

Marta and I were happy with our Orders, but I knew that trouble was brewing. I have always been a bit frightened of going too high. I have a fear of losing step with reality. I knew that the Gymnastic Federation was frustrated by our growing importance, and that Nicolae Vieru, a powerful man in Rumanian sports, had been deeply angered by the level of his award compared to mine. Even more damaging was the fact that Vieru and the Federation had lost control of the selection and coaching of the 1976 Olympic team to me.

Following the awards ceremony, I asked to immediately return to Onesti. I have always had a good instinct for knowing when I am in danger. I knew that we needed to fade from sight as soon as possible. Vieru demanded that the kids stay in Bucharest for several months to be presented at different functions. I said absolutely not. The Federation would not allow us to return to Onesti. I called Party Secretary Ilie Verdet.

Verdet invited me to his office. We had a nice chat. He told me stories about his roots and my grandfather. "Bela," he said, "you have become a legendary person, just like your grandpa." I will never forget that, it made me very proud. I felt more than pride, I felt very fortunate. It was unprecedented for a government official as high up as Verdet to take a personal interest in someone like me. It was unheard of to receive that type of attention and to have such a powerful ally. I told Verdet the situation with the Federation. He asked me what I wanted to do. I said that the only thing I wanted to do was to return to Onesti. The kids were losing sight of what was important and damage was being done. "We need to get them back to the normal life, to stop the avalanche of media and visitors,"

I explained. "You have a free hand," Verdet said. "Just tell everyone what you want to do and that's the way things will be done."

Another slap in the face of the Federation, and especially in the face of Nicolae Vieru. I returned to Onesti with the kids and laid down the law. No one was to enter the gymnasium unless I gave them specific permission. If anyone wanted to see the kids, they could watch them through the plate-glass window. I made a lot of people angry, but I thought that was the only way the kids would survive.

They did not survive.

9.

The Bear

In Rumania, survival was everything. In 1976, I saw a man get mauled to death by a bear. To understand Rumania in 1976, and to grasp the awesome power of the government and the fear it generated, is to understand why I thought twice about killing the beast, reserved exclusively to be killed by President Ceauşescu, as it unrelentingly destroyed an elderly forest ranger.

In Rumania, rank divided the culture not only economically but socially. I was not born into a high-ranking political family, and I had no political aspirations. But even the world of gymnastics turned on politics. After Ceauşescu awarded me the First Grade Order of Labor for my team's 1976 Olympic victory and Nadia's historic performance, I had the opportunity to fulfill one of my dreams: to hunt in the wild life preserve reserved for only the highest government officials.

I was invited by then Prime Minister Gheorghe Maurer to join President Ceauşescu and several other important government officials for a hunt. I was looking forward to the stillness of the air, the chill of the morning, and the thrill of the hunt. But like everything else in Rumania, the thrill of the hunt was primarily reserved for the politically elite. With the exception of a forest ranger, who had helped to organize the hunt, I was the lowest-ranking individual invited. As a result, I was placed at the periphery of the hunting line, which spread across a large ridge. The forest ranger was the only man placed farther out on the side of the ridge than myself.

It wouldn't have mattered if we had been in the dead center of the hunt. As the lowest-ranking figures involved, the ranger and I were not permitted to shoot at or kill any large game. I did not ask at the time, but I am sure nothing larger than a rabbit would have been acceptable. The large game was reserved solely for the government big shots.

Organized hunts in Rumania employed "beaters"—men with sticks who walked in a line through the woods beating the brush to drive the animals toward the ridge where the hunters silently waited. The early hours passed as I scanned the woods with my binoculars looking for game. Eventually, I caught sight of the ranger. Several hundred yards to my right, he had settled in for a nap—he knew his role in the hunt. He was propped against a large tree, his rifle resting beside him. It was then that I saw the black bear.

I will never forget the way that bear looked, his size, or his casual strength. He emerged from the tree line about 10 yards from the ranger. I watched him in silence. I watched as he lumbered toward the ranger, and I prayed that the old man would remain asleep and undetected.

If you spend enough time in the woods, you develop a sixth sense with regard to animals. Whether it is a sense of smell, sight, or hearing I do not know. But to his credit, and as a result his death, the old ranger woke abruptly. He saw the bear immediately and jumped to his feet. That was a mistake. Bears will only attack if they feel cornered, are startled, or if their young are threatened. A bear can run up to 30 miles an hour—the ranger never even had a chance to draw his gun. But I did.

I had the chance to draw my gun, and to attempt to kill the creature as he moved toward the old man. I also had the chance to be severely reprimanded by the president and prime minister of my country for killing an animal I had been forbidden to kill. All these thoughts flashed through my mind as I leapt to my feet and prepared to rush to the ranger's rescue. It seems inconceivable to most that an act of mercy, an attempt at rescue, could result in punishment. But that was Rumania, and that was my life.

In the end, I could not shoot the bear because he was on top of the ranger and my aim wasn't good enough from that far a distance. Instead, I charged toward the ranger, screaming and shooting my gun into the air repeatedly in an effort to scare off the animal. I was separated from the scene by a ravine, and remember jumping a stream and racing uphill, my view of the attack obscured for several moments. When I reached the ranger the bear was gone, lumbering back into the safety of the woods.

Even then, in the midst of the destruction that the bear had left behind, I was amazed at the creature's strength. The old man's life was barely a whisper. The bear had scalped him with one swipe, opened his body so that his vital organs were exposed, and completely severed his arm. No more than a few minutes had passed.

It was twenty minutes before anyone came to help the ranger. It was impossible to stop the bleeding—there was nothing there to hold his body together—so I held his hand. He died a few minutes later.

The hunt continued.

10.

A Great Loss

The 1977 Prague European Championship was the beginning of the end for Marta and my career, for our gymnasts, and for our school in Onesti. Thinking back now, I should have known that Vieru and the rest of the Federation would never have allowed us to survive. But back then, back then all I concentrated on were my kids, their preparation, and their successes.

The European Championship was televised, and after the 1976 Olympics everyone in Rumania was watching—including Ceauşescu. There was nothing abnormal about the competition. Ellen Berger, once the East German gymnastics coach and now part of the judging committee, was pulling strings for the East Germans. The Russians were using dirty tricks to win the gold on the vault. Nothing unusual. Nadia was performing beautifully. She was definitely going to win the individual all-round, and several of the events, still, I didn't like what was happening. I got frustrated, and I began to fight.

That was my job. I was there to fight for every score, for every thing we could turn to our favor. We lost the vault, but we won the bars and we had the two highest scores on the floor. If we fought for the scores we deserved, we might move into first place as a team. It was worth a try. I yelled, pounded, and threw my hands up in disgust at every unfair score. Things were going well. I turned to watch Nadia on the beam, and was approached by a man who said he was from the Rumanian National Council of Sports. He told me that the Rumanian government had ordered us to leave the competition.

"Leave? Why? I'm not going to walk out of competition, you've got to be really crazy, really crazy. We are going to win five out of five events. To hell with you, you damn jerk," I said, and turned back to Nadia.

Nadia came down from the beam and was awarded a 10. She was the greatest beamer I have ever seen in my career. With her performance we had the gold and silver on the beam in our pocket. There was a commotion at the main entrance. The disturbance moved over to the organizers' table. A tall, white-haired man, surrounded by a bunch of people, grabbed the microphone and began to speak. "The Rumanian delegation is to leave the arena at this very moment." It was too official to ignore. That man wasn't just from the Federation, he was from the government.

We still did not leave. The tall, white-haired man strode over to me. "I am the Rumanian ambassador. I have a mandate from Nicolae Ceauşescu, the president of the Rumanian Republic. You are to immediately evacuate." The kids all looked up at me. Dorina was about to start her routine. "Sir, what do I do?" she asked. "We have to leave," I answered sadly. We walked from the arena and were flown back to Bucharest in Ceauşescu's personal plane.

The airport was bursting with thousands of people. They were celebrating and cheering. I didn't understand. We had just been forced to leave a competition where we had been winning—

where we were virtually assured of five gold medals. What was happening?

"The president has saved the Rumanian gymnastic team from the biggest injustice ever seen in athletics," boomed a Rumanian television commentator. "Our president is a hero. . . ." You stupid jerk, my mind screamed, what are you saying? You are celebrating taking gold medals off our kids' necks. You are celebrating cheating me out of my work. You are punishing the kids, you are punishing me. . . . I could say nothing. Ceauşescu had seen me fighting for the kids and he had assumed that an injustice was occurring. He was so desperate to be a hero, to be loved by the people, that he had cheated us out of our victory. I swallowed the bitterness and returned to Onesti.

The situation was worse than our return after the 1976 Olympics, because now the kids had been irrevocably damaged. The government had sent a clear message to the team: No matter what you do, you are going to be heroes. The kids were national heroes, and they began to believe that it didn't matter whether they were good or bad, whether they were prepared or inconsistent, they would be loved.

There was a mass hysteria to see the team. They were carted all over Rumania. Function after function, party after party—it was virtually impossible to get them back into a normal life. I got tougher and tougher. I called family meetings and lectured the parents. I tried to keep the delegations out of the gym and to limit attendance at festivities. Nothing worked. Finally, I called a team meeting and tried to reach the kids.

"You are in a special position because of the disciplined life, because of the way we have been working up to this point," I said to the kids. "You are not in your current position because somebody kissed the front of your head, and overnight you turned into a different person. You guys are the same as you were before Prague; you have the same abilities, strengths, and weaknesses. If you want to keep your new status, then get back to your disciplined lives. If you want to maintain your abilities, then maintain your discipline; otherwise you will end up in a painful ditch without knowing what happened. Faster than you can imagine, you can be turned into a nobody."

I was fierce. I set up stricter rules. No family trips to endorse and promote this and that, no interruptions or disturbances in the gym, no flying to weekend government functions. I cut out everything I could. When I heard of a family party organized for foreign reporters (who always brought gifts for the kids), I stopped the party. I cleaned house and sent the kids to sleep.

I was a policeman, which I should not have had to be. And I wasn't the least bit successful. The only thing I did was create a situation that gave the Federation the opportunity to step in and be the sugar daddy. I was the mean ogre, and they were the nice people who wanted the kids to enjoy their status and privileges. I was so intent on reestablishing the norm that I didn't even see it coming.

We always had a Sunday morning workout. Sundays were our day to relax a bit, so we played games to warm up. Those games included the kids playing tricks on me. Usually they would come to practice early and hide. When I arrived at the gym they'd jump out and scare me. On that particular Sunday I arrived at the gym and it was, as usual, quiet.

"All right, all right," I said in a loud voice, "I guess nobody is here so I'm gonna go fishing." No giggles. "Well," I continued, "I guess I'll go get my poles . . ." I darted behind a storage bin and checked for hiding kids. No kids. I knew their favorite hiding place, and headed over to the pit. The pit was full of foam blocks for the kids to practice new stunts in, and they loved burying themselves in the foam. "Well," I said, "I guess before I go fishing I'm going to jump in this pit and take a nice nap." Usually they waited until I landed in the pit and then they'd beat the hell out of me with the blocks of foam. I landed—no movement, no kids. Golly, I thought, they found a new hiding place.

"I'm going to the locker room and get my old shoes for my trip," I said and raced to the lockers. I checked every damn locker, no kids. Finally I walked over to the janitor. "Have you seen my kids today?" "No," he said, "nobody has been in today but me." I looked at my watch. Today was Sunday, yes, and I had scheduled a workout, yes. Marta arrived at the gym. I said, "Did we cancel today's practice?" She said no, not as far as she knew. "Are you positive that we didn't reschedule it?"

I was about to pick up the phone and call the kids when one of our gymnasts, Georgetta, came into the gym. Georgetta had hepatitis at the time and she wasn't practicing with the team. "Georgetta," I said, "where are the others?" She began to cry. "They are gone, everybody is gone, they left only me here." Gone? Where had they gone? "Mr. Vieru and a group from the Federation were here yesterday and they went to everyone's home and packed up their belongings. They all left yesterday afternoon."

I could not believe that anybody could do such a thing without telling me. I was in charge of the team, nobody even got through the door of the gym without my approval. Georgetta's father came into the gym. "What kind of man are you," I yelled, "you did not say a word to me?" "I thought everything went through your hands," he replied.

When I arrived at the mayor's office he agreed to see me immediately. He had been a strong supporter through the years and had been instrumental in the opening of the school. "What's the problem, Bela?" he asked when he saw my face. "You let the girls go," I accused. "What are you talking about, Bela? What girls?" What girls? "Every one of my gymnasts is gone. They have been taken to Bucharest by the Federation people. They were packed up and snuck away last night." The mayor was furious. "Goddamn it, give me the phone," he roared. He called the government, he called the

Federation, no one would give him any answers. Then he turned on me.

"Your hand is in this, Bela," he yelled. What? "Don't you think I'd be happy to be coaching and hugging the girls right now," I said. "Why would I want them taken away?" We argued and yelled. We were both frustrated and mad as hell. It took several days before we learned what had truly happened.

First of all, my supporter, Ilie Verdet, was out of the country. The Federation, meanwhile, had constructed a foolproof story to cover their asses. The families, they told us, had asked to be closer to the president because it was the president's firm wish to have the team near him. There was a tiny bit of truth to that.

After I had refused to allow certain delegations into the gym, the Federation had told Ceauşescu and he had gotten extremely angry. He had made an off-hand remark that he wanted the team near him, that he wanted to watch and control them. However, never, not once, did he say that I should not be with my team. Never did he say that the Federation should steal the team, behind my back, and eliminate me as their coach. More than anything else Ceauşescu wanted positive results from the team. He knew I was the only one who could get those results.

Nicolae Vieru had finally gotten his revenge. I may have been awarded a higher honor than him in 1976, but now he had my team and there was nothing I could do to get them back. The Federation had managed to finally kick us for their own frustrations. There was nothing to do but say goodbye in our hearts to Nadia and the rest. They had never called us; their families had never contacted us. It was a bitter situation. Most of the kids had grown up in our home more than in their own. They were part of our family and now they were gone. They didn't even say goodbye.

After the team left we heard rumors. We heard that Vieru had named himself Nadia's personal coach, and that the kids were practicing in a new national gymnastics center. But they weren't practicing very much. There were different parties and functions every night. There were organized workouts, but no one could force the team to practice. I was the only one they had respected—they would never have said no to me.

We heard that Nadia was dating Nicu Ceauşescu—the son of the president, and a questionable young man. Nicu was the president of the Young Communist Organization, and we learned that he threw many parties in Bucharest for the gymnasts. They were all young, and attractive, and Nicu was a known womanizer. He was a person with no respect for athletic status, for the role models and symbols that the kids should have been.

Whenever I am hit, I fight back. I couldn't get the senior team back, but I could work with the juniors we had in Onesti, the next generation, and turn them into superstars. They were raw—they had no technical knowledge and no level of difficulty in their performances. They needed a lot of time, so I spent a lot of time with them. I stayed in the gym day and night. I held individual practices and common practices. But I could not get any momentum going.

The town had died. Most of the people in the town, not just the mayor, had been involved in our past success. They were frustrated by the turn of events and by the lack of recognition they received from the government for their efforts. That's the way it is after big results. You create a few happy people and a bunch of unhappy people. The townspeople lost interest in the school and the gym. They lost their sense of pride in our accomplishments and in their town for being a part of those accomplishments. I tried to generate enthusiasm around the young ones, to promote them, but nothing worked. Without that positive energy I couldn't create another successful team.

Marta and I agreed that we had to move away. I went to Bucharest to meet with the members of the Education Ministry. They were extremely disappointed that I wanted to leave the school in Onesti.

They had been angry when the kids were taken from us, but they believed in us and wanted us to keep trying to make the school work. I tried to explain. "The place is dead, please believe me; it is dead. I would love to stay there, Onesti is my home, but if we want to generate positive results we must move. I can't do anything more in Onesti." In the end, the Education Ministry said they would try to support me no matter what I chose to do, especially if I found a new town to start a school and gymnastics center.

When children are depressed or upset they run to their mamas. That was exactly how I felt—I wanted to return to my home, to the mining area of Rumania, and to the people who appreciated and trusted me. "Marta," I said, "we have got to go back." "How can we go back," she asked, "there is nothing there for us, there's no gymnasium, there's no facility. What would we do there?" "I don't know, Marta, but I feel like I'm going to do something there. We must go back."

In the summer of 1978, I called the regional sports organization for the mining area of Rumania. I spoke with the president of the organization, Viorel Jianu. "Bela," he said, "I want to congratulate you even though you are no longer from this area. We are all very proud of you." "Well," I said, "I am thinking about coming back home." "You crazy son of a gun," he yelled, "get back here. You will be greeted like a king!" Marta and I moved to Deva, a beautiful little town and the capital of the mining area where we both grew up. When we arrived the entire town turned out to greet us. There was a huge celebration and all the townspeople hugged and kissed us. It was such a sweet feeling. After all the frustrations, we were finally home.

11.

A Second Chance

W e've got the greatest gymnasts in the world." That's what the townspeople of Deva, and Jianu, the head of the regional sports organization, said to us during our arrival celebration. They wanted me to create another gymnastics school in their town. I tried to tell them that there were no facilities, no gymnasium, no equipment . . . "Bela, you just tell us what you want, that's all you have to do," said Jianu. I was skeptical. It would take months, maybe a year, to get enough money and support to build a gym and fill it with equipment.

The next day Jianu called a meeting at the regional Party office. The mayor, Party officials, and the directors of local industrial plants all attended. Thirty minutes later we had the money, the construction workers, and the support of the entire town to create a new gymnastics school and center. The next day the bulldozers rolled in and construction began.

The site for the gymnasium was the most beautiful part of town, right on the river valley. Above the site was a very high hill with ruins from a sixteenth-century castle on the top. Next to the site was an industrial school where carpenters had been trained. The local authorities emptied the industrial school and created a school for our gymnasts with classrooms, a cafeteria, and six small gymnasiums in the basement. It was the most perfect place we had ever worked. The town also gave Marta and me a house.

When the construction was almost completed, I received a call from the Education Ministry. "Bela," an official voice said, "congratulations, I heard that you have created a second experimental school of gymnastics." What? I said, "Wait a second, this is just a regular school for gymnastics. . . ." "Are you crazy, man," he replied. "I read a government report and the Ministry is thrilled by your efforts. We are behind you a hundred percent—we will hire the teachers for the school and you hire as many coaches as you'd like. We'll pay everyone's salaries, just organize things and then let us know what the damage is, okay?" Okay? I was so excited. I never thought the Ministry would financially back me again. Now they were giving me a free hand to create something great.

I threw myself into the school. We renovated, painted, and cleaned every damn corner and cupboard. We ordered the best equipment for the gymnasium—money was no object. Finally we held the grand opening celebration for the second experimental school of gymnastics, and then we set out to fill our school with future champions.

The selection process was much the same as it had been in Onesti. We went to elementary schools and tested kids for their interest level, flexibility, style, speed, and competitive nature. By September 15, 1977, the school was filled to capacity and we began classes and gymnastic training. One of our most promising new students was a child named Daniela Silivas. Although she was very young, we knew she was special. Daniela would later become a World and Olympic Champion.

We worked very hard with the kids. They were rough, but extremely talented. By June 1978, they had become an impressive team. We had not heard from the Gymnastic Federation for almost a year—because of our relationship with the Education Ministry, we were independent from the Federation. There was only one drawback to that independence. We would not be allowed to compete in international competitions, only national ones. There wasn't much we could do about that, so we set our sights on the National Championship scheduled for the fall of 1978.

In June 1978, I received a phone call from Nicolae Vieru. "Oh, Bela," he began, "I just wanted to call because we haven't talked for so long. I want you to know that what happened in Onesti was a big misunderstanding, a big mistake . . ." I hung up the phone.

Vieru called back several days later. "Bela," he said, "please listen to me. I am calling to let you know that we need a team to go to the Friendship Cup." The Friendship Cup is an important competition. It's for the young gymnasts, no older than sixteen, who have not yet competed in a World Championship or the Olympic Games. The Cup has always been the strongest, most aggressive, spectacular competition in the world. It's full of ambitious young gymnasts who all want to make a name for themselves.

"The Federation thought you guys might want to go to the Cup," Vieru continued. "It is being held in Cuba, and we know that we don't have much of a chance this year because your kids are young, but an international competition would be good for your team." "Why didn't you call me earlier than two weeks before the competition?" I asked. "Well, you know," Vieru responded, "an executive committee had to vote on giving your girls a chance to go over there . . ." I told Vieru that I would give him an answer later in the afternoon.

I wanted to refuse the offer, but the kids had zero competitive experience—they needed the Friendship Cup. I checked my calendar. The Cup ended five days before the Senior National Championship. That would give us enough time to fly back and travel to Bucharest for our first Senior Nationals. The Cup would be a good premeet, a good check-up and confidence builder before the Nationals. Vieru sent us one-way tickets to Cuba—he told us we could quickly schedule our return after the last day of the competition. We left for Cuba a week later.

The kids had a great competition. They won the individual and the team all-around as well as several event medals. Most importantly, they made names for themselves and set the Russian and the East German teams on their toes. They hadn't known that a team led by the Karolyis would be at the competition, and they certainly hadn't expected a new generation of Rumanian champions. Following the competition I asked our delegation leader, a good man and loyal friend, to arrange for our return.

The team attended an official banquet that night. At the end of the evening I turned to the delegation leader and asked what time our flight left in the morning. "Bela," he answered, "you're not going to believe this, but my telex to the Federation was not answered. I was on the phone all day, but all the Federation would tell me is to go to the Rumanian embassy tomorrow." I wasn't too worried, this was just another example of bureaucracy.

The next morning the delegation leader and I went to the embassy. We really needed to leave that day in order to give the kids time to prepare for the Nationals. By noontime we still hadn't seen the ambassador. By 5:00 P.M. he still hadn't appeared. I returned to the hotel to see if I could find someone to help us. All the teams had left Cuba—we were the last ones in the whole damn hotel. Even the competition's organizers had left.

At 8:00 P.M. our delegation leader returned to the hotel. I knew something was terribly wrong by the look on his face. "Where in the hell have you been?" I asked. "Bela, don't ask," he said. "We won't be able to leave this place until next week, Thursday, that's the word from the Federation." Here until next Thursday? "That's crazy," I yelled. "Next week, Monday, the Senior Nationals begin!" "Bela," he said, "I am sorry, I tried my best, I was screaming at them, fighting, but they told me that was when they could find the first available flight home for us." "Take me to the embassy," I demanded.

The ambassador allowed me to make a call to Rumania. I called Ilie Verdet. Verdet had recently been promoted to the position of prime minister of Rumania—only one position below that of Ceauşescu. President Ceauşescu had a policy called "the Rotation of the Party Leaders." He constantly shuffled individuals in high-ranking government positions in order to keep them off-balance and make sure no one became too politically powerful. In this way, he could guard against a possible overthrow.

Verdet wasn't in his office, but I told his secretary that I had an emergency, a great emergency, and that I had to talk to Verdet. Forty-five minutes later he returned my call. I had not had the chance to talk to Verdet since my team had been stolen from Onesti.

I told the prime minister how Nadia and the rest of my team had been taken away in the night, how I had started a new school, how my new team had performed in the Friendship Cup in Cuba, and how the Federation was trying to make us fly back to Rumania after the Nationals had started so that we couldn't compete. "Let me talk to the ambassador, Bela," Verdet said. As the ambassador handed me back the phone so I could speak to Verdet once again, he picked up another phone and ordered airplane tickets for our team for a flight that left the next day. "I can't thank you enough," I said to Verdet. "Bela," he responded, "you don't have to thank me for anything. I can't wait to see you guys, and I promise you that I will personally be at the Nationals."

I will never forget the look on Vieru's face when we entered the arena in Bucharest, on time, for the Senior Nationals. We were his worst nightmare. Vieru knew that if we competed in the Senior

Nationals the Federation would look bad. They had stolen the national team from Onesti. Once in Bucharest, however, they had been unable to make the kids practice. The kids had lost their discipline, stamina, size, and technical abilities. The Federation wanted to present the national team as a showcase. My team would not just show the deterioration of the national team, we would make them look pathetic. Vieru had tried to eliminate us from the competition. He thought a one-way ticket to Cuba was the answer.

When we walked into the arena the Federation people scurried around like chickens without heads. What are you doing here, how did you get back in time, they asked. I just smiled and said, "We are doing exactly what you don't want us to do. We are competing in the Senior Nationals."

After the compulsories we were in the first six places. Nadia, the star of the national team, the champion of the world, was not even competing. I thought that I caught a glimpse of her in the bleachers, but I wasn't sure because she turned her head away. I decided it couldn't have been her, because the creature I saw was the size of a monster. Still, after nine years you don't forget a look.

The optionals began the next day. Ilie Verdet entered the arena at the start of the optional competition. He was surrounded by government officials and the rest of his entourage. They sat in an honored box in the front of the gym. He found me in the crowd with his eyes and gave me a thumbs-up sign. My little guys were flying. It was just like old times. By the end of the competition we had won the first six places. Only one member of the national team had placed in the competition—Teadora Ungureanu (Dorina) had placed seventh.

Following the competition, Vieru approached me. "Bela, I want to talk to you, to explain," he began. "I want to talk to you man to man, to help you understand that in this situation we did what we had to do." "I have nothing to say to you," I replied. "Bela, don't get rough with me, just talk to me briefly, because after the awards ceremony the Federation wants to invite you to go over to Prime Minister Verdet to receive his congratulations." "You want to invite me?" I said. "Don't you feel sorry for yourself! You see that sorry national team over there, the one that is missing its greatest member, Nadia? You did that, you destroyed the careers of all those kids. You are responsible. . . ." "*No, no, no,*" Vieru yelled. "I did not know what was going to happen, I was misled. Bela, please listen to me," Vieru continued. "Your country needs you, the Federation needs you." "Vieru, why do you need me now?" I asked. "The 1978 World Championship is coming up, and we need you to get the national team in shape," Vieru began. "I am no longer the national team coach," I responded. "Tell it to somebody else, tell it to whoever is responsible for training the national team." I turned my back and walked away.

As six of our kids from Deva stood on the podium for the National Championship awards ceremony, I had such a feeling of satisfaction. We had done it again in so short a time—eight months. Under normal conditions it would have taken long years to create experienced, talented competitors. When the ceremony was over Marta and I walked hand in hand with our little gymnasts toward the locker rooms. Before we reached the doorway, I was stopped by an assistant of Verdet's. The prime minister wanted to see me. When I went over to Verdet he gave me a big hug. "You son of a gun, how in the world did you put those kids together so quickly?" he asked. "Well, you know that they are strong coal mining kids, and that area creates great people," I answered. Verdet laughed, and then he asked me to sit for a moment and talk with him.

"Bela," Verdet began, "there is a situation we must discuss. I know that the Federation has played some dirty tricks on you, but you must forget them. I want you to take our team to the World Championship in Strasbourg." "I'm sorry, I can't do that," I said. "Don't say that to me, don't say no," Verdet said. "I am your friend, Bela, I am always on your side, but we are talking about the pride

Bela, Andrea and Marta celebrate at Andrea's high school graduation. *Bela Karolyi Archives.*

Bela, Marta and choreographer, Geza Pozsar. *Bela Karolyi Archives.*

Bela and his summer camp coaches take gymnasts for a ride. *Bela Karolyi Archives.*

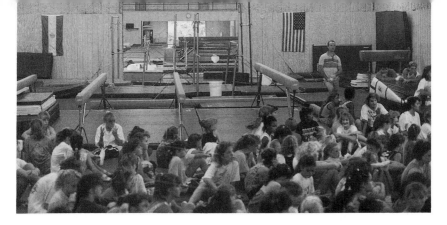

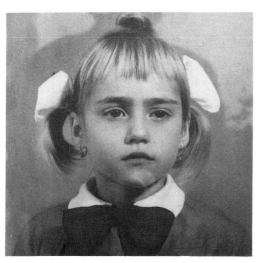

TOP: Summer gymnastic campers. ABOVE: A young Nadia. RIGHT: Nadia takes a break from her workout to give Andrea Karolyi a ride. BELOW: Andrea Karolyi and Nadia mug for the camera. *Bela Karolyi Archives.*

RIGHT PAGE: Bela hammer-throwing in high school. TOP INSET: Bela, the formidable boxer. BOTTOM INSET: Bela's parents – Nandor and Iren Karolyi. *Bela Karolyi Archives.*

Bela and Marta toast each other at their wedding dinner. *Bela Karolyi Archives.*

A strategy meeting between Marta and Bela in the early days of their coaching in Rumania. *Bela Karolyi Archives.*

The 1976 Rumanian Olympic Team. *Bela Karolyi Archives.*

Nemesis, Nicolae Vieru, stands first on the left accompanied by Bela, Marta and several gymnasts from the Rumanian team. *Bela Karolyi Archives.*

Bela, after a successful hunt in Alaska. *Bela Karolyi Archives.*

The 1973 Friendship Cup in Germany – Ellen Berger, the judge from East Germany, is on the left. *Karl-Heinz Friedrich*

ABOVE: Bela and Marta working in 1971 with the Rumanian team in Onesti. INSET: Nadia's generation outside their school in Onesti.
BELOW: The selection of young gymnasts for the gymnastics school in Deva. *Bela Karolyi Archives.*

TOP: Homecoming in Bucharest after the Montreal 1976 Olympics. From left, Marta, Bela, Nadia Comeneci, Teadora Ungureanu. ABOVE: Nadia's cute bunch in Onesti. LEFT: The graceful Teadora Ungureanu. *Bela Karolyi Archives.*

Bela's father, Nandor Karolyi. *Bela Karolyi Archives.*

Bela's grandmother at the age of 93. *Bela Karolyi Archives.*

Bela's mother, Iren Karolyi, sister Maria, and Bela. *Bela Karolyi Archives.*

of the nation and our reputation. You have helped Rumania create a status in the world and we can't have that status destroyed, no matter what mistakes the Federation has made. We are talking about our pride, and no matter how frustrated you are, you must go to the World Championship as the national team coach. I promise I will clear up the mess with the Federation, but I order you to take the national team and prepare them for the World Championship."

He had no idea what he was asking. The national team was incredibly out of shape. They had no chance of winning the Championship. He must have thought I was a magician—that I could just say hocus pocus and the national team would be in fighting form. "Prime Minister," I said, "there is no team to take. Those gymnasts are so out of shape that they cannot perform on the level of the World Championship no matter how much I work with them." "Then take your little guys," he responded. "Oh, no," I said. "Those little guys have never performed in World Championship compulsories, they have never in their lives competed in a full-scale international competition. They have no experience!" "I don't want to argue with you," Verdet said, "and you don't want to argue with me. Find a solution and report to me in a week. The competition is in Strasbourg in five weeks."

It was suicide. Marta and I returned to our hotel room and started on a bottle of Palinka. Our throats had been cut; there was no way we could create a team that the nation would be proud of and that would dominate the World Championships. We were miserable. Then I heard a small sound. I asked Marta if she'd heard something and she said no. Then I heard it again: a timid knock on the door. I yelled for the person to come in. The door didn't open. Finally I went to the door and opened it.

I knew her, but I didn't. Who was this? The face was very deformed, but when I heard the voice my stomach just dropped. "God, Nadia, is that you?" I asked. She began to cry. "I don't want to stay in Bucharest, Bela, I want to go back with you, I want to leave here." She was enormous, completely out of size. She had gained at least 40 pounds! "Nadia," I said, "you can't come back. What could you do? You are incredibly overweight, out of shape . . ." "Please, please, Bela, I want to be a champion one more time, to be good one more time in my life. Please help me."

"Nadia, do you know what you are saying? The government wants us to go to the World Championship in five weeks. Do you feel capable of going?" She said she didn't think so. "That is what I think, too," I said. "If you come back, you would have to get back into physical condition and learn new routines." "I don't care," Nadia said, "just take me back." I told her that we were no longer in Onesti, but she said she'd live in the dormitories in Deva with the rest of the team. "All right, Nadia," I said, "at least let me tell you what to expect before you make a final decision.

"If you come back with me there is absolutely no way you will get out of going to the World Championship. Ceauşescu wants you, more than anybody else, performing in Strasbourg. If you come back, dead or alive you will go to that Championship. Another thing, do you know what it means to lose thirty pounds? That's the minimum you'll have to lose in order to be able to move adequately. Your conditioning will be the ultimate torture." "I can do it, Bela," Nadia said. The next morning Nadia returned to Deva with us.

We began with an early morning run. Nadia was in such terrible shape that she could only run a few hundred yards. After a run we'd spend several hours in the gymnasium practicing, and then push the distance of her second run to half a mile. After her second run she'd have a massage, then a weight-lifting session, then a sauna, and then she'd run again. It was nonstop for hours and hours, days and weeks. I was exhausted. I did all of Nadia's training with her— I ran, coached, and ran again. In addition, I had to coach all the little guys. After a few days Nadia had lost 10 pounds, then another 5. But after two weeks she reached a plateau.

I suspected that she was sneaking food. I could run her for miles, but the weight just stuck to her. I did some detective work and found her chocolate source, which I immediately cut off. A week before the competition, Nadia reached a point where she was ready to give up. It was a horrible, horrible experience, but I did not let her off the hook. "You made a commitment, and dead or alive you will be at that Championship," I said.

The day before the World Championship, Nadia had still not completed a floor routine, though she had managed to complete a watered-down bar and balance beam routine. When we entered the arena for the podium workout the word spread fast. Nadia is out of shape, the Rumanian National team is gone, the Rumanians have no chance of winning the Championships. The Russians celebrated.

We fought like hell. Except for Nadia, the team had no experience, but those little ones put everything into their performances, beating seasoned gymnasts twice their age. And Nadia? Nadia fought for each stunt. She battled to finish each routine. She tried to compete like a champion, and at times succeeded. By the end of the competition we were still the second team in the world, and we had won seven medals—one gold for Nadia's beam routine. We were not thrilled, but we had performed to the extent of our capabilities and way above what I had realistically expected.

The atmosphere in Rumania upon our return was cold as ice. Ceauşescu was not satisfied with our results. He wanted to know what our problem was, why we had prepared so poorly, why Nadia was out of shape. It was a miracle that we had finished second as a team, that we had brought home any medals at all. Unfortunately, our president did not understand that. Of course, I was the scapegoat.

We returned to Deva. It was like returning to heaven. The whole town held a celebration. They were so proud of their little girls and their medals. They didn't care about the color of those medals, just that their kids had met with success. They automatically accepted Nadia as one of their own, and she got a lot of attention and petting from the local authorities. We immediately began to practice for the European Championship in Oslo. Nadia continued her grueling workouts, and I continued to participate in those practices as well as coach the other kids.

Five months later we swept the European Championship. The team was hot! We beat the hell out of the Russians, drove them crazy! They had expected the same team they had seen in Strasbourg—young and inexperienced. They had expected Nadia to perform poorly. But the little guys were in the best shape of their lives, and Nadia had become a totally new gymnast—tall, lean, and incredibly powerful. She had regained her focus, her drive, and the fire that had always made her a champion. In that competition, Nadia performed stunts never seen before. And she dazzled the audience with her confidence, strength, and grace. Nadia won the all-around, and was once again the European Champion. It was perhaps the greatest competition of her life.

For Marta and me it was both a beautiful competition and a moment of relief. We knew, going into that championship, that we had to produce results. Ceaușescu had voiced his disappointment with our team's performance in Strasbourg; if we didn't succeed in Oslo, it was only a matter of time before the Federation found a way to step in. If we didn't produce results, we would lose our team and perhaps our school once again. Winning the European Championship placed us in momentary control, and allowed me to focus on preparing my team for their next big international competition: the World Championships in the United States.

12.

Nadia Continued

T he optional portion of the 1979 World Championship in Fort Worth, Texas, was only moments away from beginning. Nadia was sitting in the bleachers with her hand bandaged—the result of Nicolae Vieru's interference. The rest of our team, five tiny gymnasts who had lost their leader and their confidence, practically shook with fear. I knew that I had to turn the situation around.

I looked at the long, desperate faces of my gymnasts and knew that concentration was gone. They would make childish mistakes on simple things. We had only minutes before the competition was to begin, and we were only five people. That meant that each score counted—the lowest score could not be discarded, as was the practice with six competitors.

In competition, the first performer is the sacrificial lamb. Traditionally the scoring starts out low, and the first gymnast must try to get the highest score possible so that her teammates can improve upon her performance and build up their scores. So the first gym-nast's score is vital. We had lost our margin for error. Even our first performer had to achieve a high score. I shut out the sound of the Russian team celebrating our misfortune and turned to my team.

"Okay, guys," I said, "this is going to be just another good meet." They looked at me as if I had lost my mind. I smiled a big smile and began, "First of all, I'd like to ask you, what is your name?" One of the little ones whispered her name. "All right, very good, you know your name! And what about you, and you, and you," I said. They all whispered their names. "Very good, you all know your names, you son of a guns. I guess we're in pretty good shape!"

"Now listen up," I said, "you've complained all along that you cannot win a damn competition because of Nadia. Well, now Nadia's gone and it's all yours. You can win the floor, beam, bars, and vault. You can win the individual all-around as well as the team all-around title. Go for it, dammit! If you want to prove that you've been working hard, preparing hard, then go out there and eat them up. Are you afraid of those suckers? Are they better than you? Have they worked harder than you? I guarantee you that nobody, nobody worked harder for this competition than you have. You have the right to compete, with or without Nadia, you have the right. It doesn't matter whether or not we win. Do your best. Can we do it?" The team began to cheer. "Okay then, let's go get those god-damn son of a guns."

First event, uneven bars. First score 9.8, second score 9.9, third score 10, fourth 10, fifth 10. The kids were flying. I turned to Nadia after our fifth gymnast had performed and told her to go up and touch the bar. She said, "Sir, I cannot do anything." I said, "You just go up and touch the bar, present yourself, and come down." She did not ask me why, she just did as I said. And, at the time, I could not have told her why. I didn't really know. I just knew that keeping Nadia in the competition might help somewhere down the line.

Nothing could stop the kids. They were on fire—flying through their events with higher and higher scores. Nadia presented herself on each piece of equipment without performing. Then came the beam. We started with a 9.75, then a 9.85, third 9.9, fourth 9.9. The fifth performer was to get a 10—the stage had been set, the scores had been built up. But our fifth little gymnast had no experience.

My best strategy has always been to create a star, a winner, the one who could, by her training, personality, and nature, hold and carry the pressure. But our little girl fell off the beam. She broke under pressure. At the same time the Russians won the floor event.

Everything was lost. Even though we had climbed to a 9.95 on the beam, we were lost. I looked up at the scores and made some calculations, then I turned to Nadia.

I was so frustrated that I couldn't speak, but I looked at Nadia, and I said in my mind, "Nadia, did you ever think that you had any obligations to your team members? I have to tell you that you do have obligations, 'cause all these little guys carried all the hard parts of your victories. These are the ones who built your scores for so many years. These are the ones who have never been recognized for that. These are the silent soldiers who carried the hard part of your glory.

"Did you ever think that you owed me or Marta anything for what has happened over the years? If you truly feel that for all our work and consideration you owe us something, then walk up right now and do a beautiful thing . . . do your beam routine." I knew she would say that she couldn't even get up on the beam. Yes you can, I thought. You can do your full-press handstand with one hand and a few fingers from your other hand. You don't have to put all your weight on your bad hand. You can do layouts and one-handed handsprings and a simple round-off double full-out dismount. I wanted to tell Nadia all of this, but I couldn't, because I didn't truly believe she could successfully perform.

Nadia did not say a word as I stared at her. She just looked into my eyes and then turned toward the beam.

The green light went on and Nadia walked up to the beam. I will never forget that moment. I was facing away from the beam, waiting to hear the public's reaction. I couldn't look—I thought Nadia might turn around and never start her routine. Even if she did start, I was 90 percent sure that she would fall. Silence. Total silence in the arena. I turned around.

There was Nadia, one hand and three fingers from the other hand on the beam, moving slowly, perfectly, into her handstand, quarter turn-out, step-out, and then the familiar rhythm of her beam routine. She threw her first back handspring, one-handed of course, then layout, layout—a powerful routine, beautiful. When she threw her dismount she stuck it! And at that moment all hell broke loose in the arena. It was so obvious, with her big bloodied bandage, that she was injured, and therefore so incredible that she had performed a near-perfect one-handed routine. The public went wild. The score came up, 9.95. We were back in first place.

Nadia quietly walked back to the bleachers. She had made her contribution to the team's victory. What she did not realize at the time was that she had just written an unforgettable page in the history of gymnastics about courage, dedication, and the spirit of sacrifice of a young human being.

The kids were so pumped up that there was no way to stop them. Nadia could not compete in the rest of the events, but it didn't matter. The little guys were flying high. Nobody could touch them. The tens kept coming all in a row. And then it was over and we had won our first all-around team title in a World Championship. And the Russians? It was like someone had died in their corner of the arena.

13.

The Communist Olympics

Three weeks after the World Championship in Texas, Nadia told Marta and I that she wanted to move back to Bucharest. I said, "If that is your peace then go, but remember that time is short before the 1980 Olympics and you must maintain your momentum and standards."

I understood Nadia's desire to return to Bucharest. She was at that age, nineteen, a grown-up young woman. When you're nineteen, your heart starts to beat when you think about somebody special. At the gymnastics school Nadia was the star, the older one—she didn't quite fit into the atmosphere. Nadia had already accumulated all the years of training and style we were working on with the rest of the team. Her training was different—quality, not quantity. We worked on shaping and polishing, on maintaining tricks, skills, and condition. The rest of the team was on a totally different type of regimen. I wasn't surprised that Nadia left.

A few months before the 1980 Olympic Games—the first all-

Communist Games due to the fact that the United States and others were boycotting the event because of the Russian invasion of Afghanistan—Nadia called me and asked if she could return. She was not as out of shape as before, but her endurance and strength were gone. Less conditioning and intensity in workouts hadn't helped her maintain her shape.

We started to work. Things didn't go badly, but Nadia had changed. Her level of enthusiasm was not as high as it had been in 1977 or 1979. She was not fighting as she had after Strasbourg. It was a flat attitude, not negative; she was missing the flame. I could tell that the fire was no longer there.

Nadia had spent time in the big city, the high-society atmosphere, and her mind was filled with new interests and priorities. Athletic training took second place now—in the past it had always dominated. Still, we went to Moscow for the 1980 Olympic Games. There was no question in my mind that Nadia would once again win the all-around title. She was in good shape, and her reputation would help her. There was no question in my mind that unless Nadia made a major mistake no one could take that title away from her.

When we entered the arena in Moscow for the official presentation of teams we were met with a horrible booing. I mean a booing from all over, just all over. I thought that perhaps this was the Russian way of applauding. Then I heard the jeers and whistles. What in the hell was going on? We had never experienced anything in gymnastics like that. I had never heard one person booing, and this was hundreds, maybe thousands of people booing. I looked into the bleachers and saw soldiers everywhere. Soldiers booing . . . who were they booing?

The presentation ended and it was time for the teams to begin competition. We walked out onto the floor with three other nations. The first two teams entered the arena to wild applause. Then Rumania entered, and that horrible booing began again. That's when I realized that we had been set up. Not only was the booing for us, but the Russians had expressly placed their military in the audience to disturb us.

I looked into the bleachers and watched the soldiers, fingers in their mouths, whistling and booing. I ran over to the organizers and said, "What in the hell is going on here?" I was told that the audience could do anything they wanted. I did not argue. I wanted to keep my eyes on the little ones, my kids.

You cannot race like a horse when you are booed. The kids had trouble concentrating and focusing on their compulsory routines. Regardless of their performances, regardless of their scores, they left each event to boos and jeers. I wanted to scream at the audience, to say, "Hey, you bastards, these are just young ladies and you are hurting them. Hurt me, don't hurt my kids."

Going into the optionals we were in second, behind the Russians. It was a comfortable position—close enough to pull ahead. Ellen Berger was the head of the technical committee, and several times I protested scores. Not surprisingly, I got no results. The all-around competition continued. It was a nightmare, scores missing, scoring controversies, more yelling, more booing. Finally we reached the last event.

The way the rotation worked, the beam was our designated final event. For the Russians, it was the bars. Yelena Davydova was the Russians' only hope of beating Nadia. She was their only competitor who had not made a major mistake. Davydova was scheduled to perform sixth on the bars. Nadia was scheduled to perform second on the beam.

The first beam competitor, a Spanish girl, performed her routine. Her scores came up and then it was Nadia's turn. The judges began to confer. I watched the Russian judge talking, but his eyes were on the bars. The second competitor began her bar routine. The third competitor completed her bar routine. Still the judges for the beam were in conference. Still Nadia waited on the floor to begin her beam routine.

I called Nadia back to me and gave her a little massage. I told her to do some walkovers and jumps to warm up. Finally, the judges appeared to have finished their conference and took their seats. Nadia once again readied herself to perform. In the meantime, I looked over at the bars and saw that the fourth performer was in the middle of her routine. What was going on? The flag for Nadia to begin was still not up.

I went over to the grand jury and asked what was happening. Nobody answered me. The fifth performer had now completed her bar routine and the sixth competitor, Davydova, had begun her routine. I turned to watch the young Russian perform. Davydova had reduced her chances of error by taking out the major difficulty. As her feet hit the mat, almost simultaneously, a score of 9.95 flashed across the board. They might as well have put up the score before Davydova performed.

The green flag went up, and Nadia finally began her beam routine. A routine that was solid like a rock, an unquestionable 9.95 if not a 10. The judges began to confer. They huddled together, and spoke in whispers. Finally Nadia's score flashed across the screen—9.85. I knocked the damn scoreboard down.

Chaos! The Russian head judge jumped up and yelled at me to stay away. "Stay away," I roared, "*No way!* I want to see the individual judges' scores, I demand to see the scores." The judges, from Czechoslovakia, Poland, Bulgaria, and the Soviet Union, had arranged to have Davydova perform her bar routine before Nadia so they could make sure Nadia's score was sufficiently less than Davydova's to ensure the gold for Russia. They had delayed Nadia's scoring until they had figured out what score should be given to make Davydova the winner. And they wanted me to stay away? I was beyond furious.

Yuri Titov was the head of the jury of appeal, and the executive director of the International Gymnastics Federation. He was the top person in the FIG. I ran over to Yuri. "How can you let this happen?" I said. "You used to be a gymnast, how can you let this thing happen in the eyes of the whole world? How can you compromise the Olympic spirit in this way?" He appeared upset, and he assured me he would make things right.

Titov called down to the judges and told me he directed them to change Nadia's score to a 9.90. He told me that Nadia would be the individual all-around champion. But Titov was a poor mathematician. He thought that by changing Nadia's score, Nadia and Davydova would be tied for first place. I did not know that was his plan, I only knew that according to my calculations Nadia had won the all-around Olympic Championship—a few hundredths of a point ahead of Davydova. "Okay, old friend, are you happy now?" Titov asked. "Yes, yes, I am happy," I said.

The competition was over and it was time for the awards ceremony. The kids lined up. Davydova, Nadia, and Gnauck. They began their procession toward the awards platform. Then I noticed the flags. On the left, the Rumanian flag; in the middle, the Russian flag; on the right, the East German flag. That is not right, I thought, if my flag is on the left it cannot be the winning flag. The winner has got to be in the middle. Something was wrong.

I watched the flags as the orchestra started. The flags all rose to the same place and then *whoop*, the Russian flag continued to rise and the Rumanian flag remained at the same level as the East German flag. "Oh, no you don't," I yelled. "Nadia get back here." Nadia turned away from the podium and walked off the floor.

That's when it really got crazy. People were running everywhere. Titov approached me fuming with anger. "What in the hell are you doing, Bela?" he screamed. I said, "This is a disgusting cheating game, and you were the orchestrator." Titov said he'd made a mistake, that there could not be a tie for first place. The scoreboard for Nadia's beam routine rose again—9.85—I knocked it down once more.

For forty minutes the scandal continued in front of the spectators. Finally we just walked out of the awards ceremony. As I was leaving, an ABC affiliate reporter came over to me and stuck a microphone in my face. He asked what I thought of the competition. I told him that frankly I'd never seen anything so unjust, so corrupt, or so lacking in the spirit of the Olympics. I told him I could not recognize this part of the sport of gymnastics—devoid of fairness and appreciation. My comments were shown on Rumanian television.

Upon returning to our hotel we were barraged with calls from Rumania (citizens, not government officials), of congratulations. "We are behind you guys, we are totally supportive," they said. It was a revolution.

For forty years, Rumania had been dominated by the Russians and by communism. For forty years no one had ever attempted to oppose the Russians, or the Communist directives. Now here it was, the Olympic Games in Moscow, the heart of the Communist system, and a hot-headed Rumanian coach had stopped the Games for forty minutes, protested, knocked down scoreboards, and called back his athletes from the awards ceremony.

In the heart of the Soviet Union, during the first all-Communist Olympic Games, I had unwittingly become the leader of the people. A people who were all crying in unison, "We don't want Russian domination. We don't want to bow our heads and lay down in front of the Russians, we no longer accept the humiliation." In forty minutes we had become national heroes and political symbols.

Marta and I spent the next three days celebrating—reading letters and telegrams from friends and supporters. We could hardly wait to return home to greet the people and to be part of another post-Olympic celebration. We flew into the Bucharest airport and as the door of our plane opened we braced ourselves for the cheers of the people and the celebrations that awaited us.

No one was there. We knew from the calls and letters that the Rumanian people supported us, but for some reason the police had stopped the flow of traffic to the airport. We had no idea why, only that something had gone wrong. From the airport we traveled directly to Deva.

Two days later I received a memorable phone call from the Communist Central Committee. A very official voice said, "Tomorrow morning, at first hour, be in Bucharest and report to the Central Committee . . . by order of President Nicolae Ceauşescu."

If the Democrats were the only party in the country, and they had a powerful headquarters where men from their party could decide at the drop of a hat whether you were alive, dead, or imprisoned, that would be the Central Committee. They had total control over the government, every institution, and every man, woman, and child. This was not the first time I had been summoned.

I was not worried. Although the people had not come to support us at the airport, they had been more than supportive upon our return to Deva. We were feeling like heroes—loved and admired. And it wasn't uncommon to be summoned to the Committee headquarters after an international competition.

I thought the call was an invitation to help the members of the Central Committee plan a celebration similar to the ones after previous Olympic Games. In the past, these celebrations involved high government officials. The president gave out distinctions and honors, and monetary awards to the gymnasts' families. I wasn't worried about the meeting because we had, in fact, been waiting for this call from the government.

The man who usually conducted the sports-related meetings at the Central Committee was Ilie Verdet. I was looking forward to giving him my report and discussing the format of the celebration. In the past, Verdet usually wanted to meet at lunchtime, so we could spend a few quiet moments talking without being disturbed. This time I had to be there at 8:00 A.M.

I knew all the guards at the Central Committee office, and on that morning I greeted each one, especially my favorite, a colonel named Popa. "Hi, Popa," I said, "how are you doing?" He didn't respond. "Well," I said, "I'm going up to see the boss." "No," he barked, "you've got to wait over in the hall until you are called." I said, "Popa, is the boss not here today?" He didn't answer.

So I waited, and waited and waited. I stood for three hours. At 11:00 A.M. a man came down and signaled for me to follow him. I was then left to wait in the secretary's area just outside Verdet's office. I had known Verdet's secretary for a long time, and I asked her what was going on. "Is anything wrong?" I said. She answered, "I don't know, I don't know if anything is wrong." She wouldn't look me in the eye. And she never warned me that my supporter, Verdet, had been "shuffled" by Ceauşescu and was now an ambassador—a demotion that made him virtually powerless in the government. Then I heard a voice say, *Drag him in,* and I knew something was indeed terribly wrong.

Verdet was not there. There were seven or eight people at a long conference table. I said hello, but no one looked up or answered. I assumed that everyone was waiting for the boss, Verdet, and moved toward the side of the room where there was a chair. *"You stay there, you stay on your feet,"* one of the men barked at me. This is bad, I thought, I'm really in some kind of trouble. At that point I still had no idea what I had done.

"Tell us what happened at the Moscow Olympic Games," a small, fat man with glasses asked. I asked what he was talking about. *"Don't ask questions, just answer me,"* he said. "Well," I said, "if you are talking about the protest, the judging controversy, or the cheating, I tried to stop it. I tried to turn the event around and to defend the rights of the kids and of Rumania." "Don't tell us tales," the man continued. *"Who told you to disturb the first Communist Olympic Games? Who gave you permission to talk to the Western media?*

Who the hell do you think you are? How could you say to the world that our friends, our Soviet friends, were cheating?"

"Excuse me," I began, "I was in Moscow for only one reason, to defend the rights of my gymnasts. I was there to defend their chances, under very difficult circumstances, to acquire the honors and awards they deserved. To defend the right of the athletes and the purity of the sport. And that was the only thing that I did in Moscow. I fought for the kids, for my country, and for the right to exist and succeed in a decent situation."

"You are not impressing us with your speeches," the fat little man spat toward me. *"You embarrassed us in the eyes of the West and you humiliated and disturbed our Soviet friends."* "I was the one who was helpless," I said. "I was not a soldier screaming insults and throwing food. I did not have an army behind me or a gun in my hand. I had only my words and my convictions, but I still fought injustice."

"Let's talk about your comments to the Western media," said a man seated at the middle of the table. I had never met this young man before, but I was sure that he was Nicu Ceauşescu, the president's son. Nicu had been romantically linked to Nadia in the past, and I knew our goals for Nadia and our pull on her were in direct opposition. I had heard that Nicu hated me, and that he had tried to stop Nadia from returning to my school in Deva. Nicu was intent on flouting his father's power and living a life without purpose or discipline. He was his father's chosen successor.

I explained to Nicu that my comments were on the cheating that was going on, and the manipulatory judging. I also told him that I had said that what was happening in the bleachers, the jeering and booing, was not ethical or decent. That in gymnastics there had always been an appreciation for the discipline and beauty of the sport. Nicu just sneered at my answer.

The fat man began again, *"Let me tell you, you have humiliated Rumania. You have cast a shameful shadow on the first Communist*

Games and insulted our greatest friends. I had to receive comments from the Soviet government about your irresponsible actions. You gave wind to the wheel of the Western media and a picture of our Olympics just as they wished to see them—full of disturbances and compromises." I looked at the man and knew that there was nothing more I could say. *"I am going to throw you in jail, hide you forever; you will never see the light of day,"* he screamed.

The fighting was over. I had staked my reputation and defended my actions against their stupidity as best I could. "I have no more comments . . . I resign," I said, and I turned and left the room. As I left, I heard one of the men shout, *"You don't need to resign—you are nothing anymore!"*

Now I was scared. As soon as I got into the corridor I turned around to see who was following me. No one was in the hallway. So I walked as quickly as I could past the elevator and down the staircase. I assumed that security had been called and that there would be armed guards waiting at the front door. As I walked past Popa I expected to feel his large hand on my neck, pushing me to the ground. Nothing happened. I looked over my shoulder; Popa and the rest of the guards were busy talking. As soon as I was on the street I thanked God for letting me see the sun one last time.

Well, they must have decided not to create a scene at the Committee office, I thought. They are probably going to let me walk around the corner and then they will grab me. Please, God, I asked, give me a chance to get to my car—at least then I can give them a good chase. I walked hurriedly, and finally spied my car in the distance. There were no guards anywhere. I crossed the street and began to circle through the blocks. Finally I reached my car and jumped into the driver's seat. Please, God, I wished, let me one more time go home and see Marta and my little daughter, Andrea.

I knew a lot of shortcuts around Bucharest and back to my town. I took every farm and side road I knew on that drive. I did not get home until after dark. I didn't drive up to the house because I thought there would be secret police waiting for me there. I was afraid they would drag me away before I had a chance to say goodbye to my wife and daughter. So I parked on another street and jumped the back fence of my house.

I knocked on the back window for Marta. "What's going on, Bela? Why aren't you coming in the front door?" she asked as she let me into the house. I told her that I was most likely going to be picked up by the police very soon. Marta listened in silence. "Please try to do the best you can with Andrea," I said. "Apply for a teaching job rather than coaching . . . we can no longer coach . . ." We sat for hours making plans and saying goodbye. I called my parents and asked them to take care of Andrea on the off-chance that Marta, too, was picked up. We weren't sure, even though the actions in Moscow had been mine alone, whether Marta would also be blamed.

Nothing happened. We waited inside our home the whole next day. Finally I decided to go to the gym in Deva—I thought a public place might be the safest. I coached for three days before I was summoned by the local authorities. My friend and supporter, Viorel Jianu, spoke to me in confidence. "We know what happened in Bucharest," he began, "and we still support you. You made a political mistake, but we appreciate all you've done. You must be very careful now, Bela, they are after you."

So nothing happened. Nothing except that the Gymnastics Federation immediately stepped in. The first thing they did was cut the part of our budget that came from them. At the time we had a combined budget—part from the Federation, part from the Education Ministry. The Federation portion was drastically reduced and the Education portion was also decreased. We could no longer meet the financial requirements of the school.

One by one people left. The local authorities tried to help, but it was difficult because they had to hide their support. No one could openly give us assistance. I tried to lobby the industrial plants and organizations in the community, and they quietly sent us food and gasoline, but I knew this type of help could not continue. Inside, I knew we would not be able to go on much longer. Finally I told Marta that things were just getting worse and worse. We were going to have to think about closing the gymnastics center and applying for regular teaching jobs. This was a very low point in our lives.

It's strange, but even at the lowest points, even at the prospect of starting over once again, neither of us ever considered defection. We were fighters. Naturally we assumed we were going to succeed again.

I never considered running away and giving up everything. Through the years we had saved enough money to buy our own home—completely paid for—and that happened very seldom in Rumania. We had a six-year-old daughter, and the thought of putting her at risk was unacceptable. Things were still not that bad for us; I knew we could turn our situation in Rumania around again.

I was wrong.

14.

Doomed

Five months after the 1980 Olympic Games, our gymnastics school in Deva had lost most of its personnel. During this time we were never contacted by the Federation. It seemed that they had lost interest in us. After all, Nadia had already gone back to Bucharest. From time to time we heard about her and some of her former teammates. There were many special events and celebrations for Nadia and her fellow gymnasts. We heard bits and pieces, but we were too busy trying to stay afloat to pay much attention.

In December 1980, we were forced to pay attention. I received my first phone call from the Central Sports Committee since my meeting at the Committee headquarters. "Bela," a man said, "we are organizing an American tour to raise money for the Federation. Make sure that your gymnasts are in good shape and are ready to perform." "You have made a mistake," I answered, "I am no longer the national team coach. I have no national team responsibilities—

I gave my resignation months ago." "There was no resignation accepted," he said. "And as long as you are eating the bread of the country you had better comply with your obligations." "My obligations?" I yelled into the phone, "I have fulfilled my obligations to the kids, the community, and my country to the maximum extent." I hung up the phone.

That call was followed by another the next day. This time the call came from the Central Party Committee. I could not recognize the voice, but the message was clear: "Get the kids together and be ready to leave for an exhibition tour in the United States in two weeks. You are going on a twenty-five day, twenty-city exhibition tour. Be careful over there, behave yourself, get the money and come home."

I tried to object. "Sir," I said, "I'm sorry, but I don't have any involvement in this tour. I have not been in contact with the national team. I'm just working at the school in Deva with young gymnasts. Most of the gymnasts that the Americans would be interested in are in Bucharest. You have called the wrong person." "We are talking and you are listening from now on," he responded. "You had better get used to our orders, and you had better do what we say if you want to smell the roses on a free status basis. This is an order, do you understand?" "Yes," I said, "I understand."

"What in the world are we going to do?" I asked Marta. "We have no choice, there is no alternative," she replied. So I turned to the task of organizing the tour. I called the Federation to speak to the man in charge of the exhibition: Nicolae Vieru.

Vieru's tone was cold and official. "I have a mandate from the government to put together this exhibition tour to raise a minimum of $180,000 for the Federation. I am the leader of the delegation, and I am fully responsible for its success. Bela, you are under my direct supervision, and you are not to speak to anyone in America unless I say it is all right." Vieru continued to speak, but I stopped listening. This was just one more situation I would have to get through. I tried to swallow the sour taste in my mouth.

Vieru informed me that he was going to bring Nadia on the trip. I was to bring seven additional gymnasts from my school. I organized the kids, and together with Marta and Geza Pozsar (our choreographer and dear friend) we traveled to Bucharest. Andrea, our daughter, remained in Deva with my old aunt. It was January 1981 when we met Vieru and Nadia at the Bucharest airport. The executive director of the Rumanian Gymnastic Federation swept toward us.

"I am Nicolae Vieru," he said to the kids, "and I have a mandate from the government to conduct this exhibition for the Federation. I want to make it clear that no one has the right to make comments, give interviews, or take any individual action on this tour without my approval." Vieru turned and began to introduce the enormous men standing behind him.

I couldn't help laughing. Vieru was introducing the muscle-heads behind him as journalists. One of those journalists was a secret policeman from Deva. He was an ordinary bastard, not even worth spitting on. I laughed and said to him, "I didn't know you changed professions, when did you become a journalist?" Quickly Vieru pulled me aside. "We don't want your comments, watch your mouth," he said. "These men are journalists, period." Then Vieru looked me directly in the eye, "We have four such men on the tour, do you understand?" I told him I understood.

It was clear from the start how the tour would run. As our group moved toward the passport station, the four "journalists" shadowed Marta, myself, and Geza. No matter what we did, step left, step right, go to the bathroom, they were with us. In every hotel our guards had rooms directly across from ours. Their doors were always open. They were always watching. The ensuing tour was a nightmare. We could not talk to anyone—it was frustrating and humiliating.

Following each exhibition, American journalists would ask me for a few comments. Without fail, before I could open my mouth, Vieru would jump in and grab the microphone. "What do you want to know?" he would shout. "I am the one who answers here, I am the executive director of the Rumanian Gymnastics Federation." I remember thinking to myself God, God, God, what a jerk!

All I wanted was for the tour to end. To go back home and end the nightmare. Marta and I had decided that when we returned we would apply for teaching positions with the Education Ministry. We were going to try to move back to Vulcan, where we knew there would always be an open door.

The only high point of the tour was the opportunity to see my old friend Paul Ziert. Paul was (and still is) Bart Conner's coach. Throughout the years, Paul was the only American coach who tried to communicate with us. He had become our dear friend. Although neither of us spoke the other's language, we communicated through facial expressions and gestures, food and drink, and the international language of friendship. Over the years, Paul had learned that I was an avid hunter, and that more than anything in life I wanted a real bird dog. In the middle of the tour, he surprised me with a beautiful dog. That type of thoughtfulness and generosity was typical of Paul. I remember that I couldn't wait to fly that dog back home and show him off to my friends.

The tour ended in New York City. We were all invited to the Rumanian embassy for a celebratory dinner. Marta and I were looking forward to seeing the ambassador. On a previous trip to New York he had met us at the airport with his entire family, and they had given us a tour of the city. As we walked into the embassy everyone was greeted personally by the ambassador and his wife. The kids were hugged, and Vieru was congratulated on the success of his tour. Marta, Geza, and I were not greeted.

We were invisible throughout the cocktail hour. Finally, everyone was invited to sit down at the long dinner table. Surprise, surprise, there were three place settings missing. Marta, Geza, and I were seated on the side of the room. There was no room at the table for us. The evening continued. Vieru made speeches in which the three of us were never acknowledged. The ambassador, the same fellow who had pretended to be our best friend during our last visit, who had said things like "my home is your home" to us in 1976 and 1977, did not acknowledge our presence the entire evening. The only attention we received were suspicious smiles, whispers, and looks.

That night in our hotel room the three of us drowned our fears and misery in Palinka. We drank to the end of the tour. "Cheers," we said, "we finally get to go home to our families." Geza drank to seeing his wife and child, we drank to seeing Andrea. The hell with the Federation and the government, we said. We don't want anything to do with those bastards anymore! There was a knock on the door.

We thought it was one of the kids. I told them to come in. Vieru walked through the door. He was smiling, and asked if he could join us for some Palinka. What the hell, I told him to grab a glass. I poured some into his glass and he began to talk in a soft friendly voice. "I wanted to talk to all of you. We have known each other for a very long time, and, ah, I just wanted to tell you that I have always admired you. You have to understand that even though politically I am your boss, and you are under my directions, I have always appreciated you so much. I, ah, love you guys . . . you know that."

None of us were buying any of Vieru's speech, but we continued to listen. "Because we are such old friends, I wanted to come and talk to you about something. You know, ah, that if you ever want to leave the country, to defect, you have to do it very quietly. I don't know if you know this, but those four men with us are from

the secret police. They've been watching and following all of you—
me, too! They report everything. Last night they reported to me
that you guys are planning to defect, to go to California. I love you
guys, but you've got to be more discreet in the future. Forget your
plans to defect, that is over now. You have been caught. The
problem now is the media. I've talked to the ambassador and he is
going to help us avoid the American media at the airport."

We couldn't believe what we were hearing. What the hell was
he talking about? Vieru continued, "I am sorry to say this, but it
was my obligation to report your attempt to defect to the ambassador. But I am your friend, and when we return I'll tell the officials
that nothing ended up happening. Remember, in the future though,
my friends, that if you want to defect you must be much more
discreet."

He said all this with a straight face, a sincere face. His voice was
soft, smooth, and confidential, but it was the voice of a snake. "*You
bastard!*" I roared. All my blood was pounding in my head. Geza
started to yell, "*What are you saying? What are you insinuating?*"
Marta didn't yet comprehend what had happened.

This was the dirtiest setup anyone could have imagined. There
was Vieru, most likely wired for recording, trying to get us to admit
that we had planned to defect. Regardless of what we said, no
matter how much we denied his lies, Vieru would be the hero. We
would return to our country, attempted defectors, and Vieru would
be the savior, the one who had learned of our plans and notified
the government.

"*Get out of this room, you goddamn bastard!*" I screamed. Vieru
jumped to his feet and retorted, "I see you are getting excited, but
you should have been nice to me. I was going to defend you, but
now I won't even do that." I lunged at him, but the door opened
and one of our large "journalists" pushed me back inside the
room.

We sat and looked at each other. We had no words. "I knew

this was going to happen," Marta cried. "They were after us." Geza said nothing. We sat in silence for hours. Finally we began to talk. We listed all the pros and cons. If we go back, what will we face? If we don't go back, what will we face? Marta and my biggest concern was Andrea. If we returned she would be the child of convicted criminals. She would live under the stigma of political wrongdoing—in Rumania, there was nothing worse. If we did not return, would we be able to bring her to the United States? Geza also had his wife and daughter to think about.

Geza had studied some international law in Rumania. He told us that legally the government could not stop our children or his wife from coming to the United States. But we still did not know how exactly we would get them out. All we knew for sure was that our government would be very angry, and they would not hesitate to take that anger out on our families. We would not be made to look like heroes, like the lucky ones who got away. The Rumanian government would never accept looking foolish.

Marta and I talked in circles. If we defected it might be difficult, or impossible, to get Andrea to the United States. If we didn't defect we might never see her again anyway—we would most likely be picked up at the airport and locked in some prison. What in the world were we going to do?

What if we decided to defect? We knew no English, had few friends to turn to in the United States, didn't know how to secure immigrant status or a green card . . . Hell, we didn't even know how to use the telephones. We were in one of the largest most frightening cities in the United States. We had approximately three hundred American dollars, and a bird dog named Butts.

As the morning light crept beneath the blinds of our hotel room, we looked into each other's tired eyes and saw the answer. There was no return.

That morning there was a short shopping trip scheduled for the gymnasts. They were each given a little money to buy gifts for friends and family. I decided that, in my own way, I had to say goodbye to my kids. I had known most of them since they were three or four years old, and I had known Nadia for what seemed a lifetime.

Around 7:00 A.M. I called the kids to a meeting in the reception area. I looked at them, and I had difficulty beginning. I had never had to say goodbye to them before. I had never considered the possibility of leaving them. I didn't want them to think that I had deserted them, or that I had run away. I wanted them to know that I had to leave, was forced to leave. Today, I still wish I could have told them all those things, but at the time, I could not put our plans in jeopardy.

"Well guys," I began, "this is our last morning in New York, and you are going to do a little shopping. Make sure that you are back by ten A.M. because you leave for the airport at eleven. I want to remind you of something before you go home. I want to remind you that the satisfaction you have had from competition, and all the success and glory that you have accumulated and experienced over the years, came only for one reason—because you put in tremendous efforts and lived a disciplined life with a strict physical and mental regime. That is what made you tremendous athletes, and that is the only way you will maintain your success. Never forget that only hard work and the disciplined life can lead to the type of satisfaction that you are now experiencing."

I looked into their little faces and continued. "I know that you are happy now. The tour is over, and you have a little money to buy a few things for your families. But remember that all these exhibition tours are still generated by athletic results, and those results will never come without very hard work." The kids began to look at me strangely. They knew something was different. I had given pep talks before, when needed, but the tour was over and we were going home.

"Make sure," I concluded, "that no matter what your steps are, or in which arena in life you ultimately decide to practice, that you are disciplined and strong people. Now you are free to do some shopping." Most of the little ones went running out the door. A few lingered to talk for a moment. Nadia stayed.

"Bela, what do you mean?" Nadia quietly asked. "Nadia," I answered, "I am not going back." She began to cry. "I don't want to go back either, let me stay with you," she begged. "Nadia, I cannot take that responsibility. I am here in the middle of nowhere, surrounded by strange people who speak a language I do not know. I don't know where I am going to eat or sleep tomorrow. I don't even know what I am going to do tomorrow, but I'm a grown person and I have to take whatever comes. I can't guarantee you a decent life or a safe and quiet environment here. I can't even guarantee that for Marta and me."

Nadia continued to cry softly. I said, "Listen to me, Nadia. You are only twenty years old. You must go back and finish college. After college you will have a diploma in your hand that you can lean on. When you have that diploma you can make a decision on your own. If you stay here everyone in the world will think that I kidnapped you, that I made you stay and go through the nightmare that we are most likely going to face." "You can't leave me, you can't," Nadia said. "It's not the right time, Nadia," I said. I loved Nadia, but I would never have willingly placed her in our desperate situation. Vieru and the guards walked into the room.

"Nadia," I whispered, "please don't cry in front of these people. Don't tell them anything." Vieru walked over to us. "What is going on here? Nadia, what is wrong?" he asked. She replied that nothing was wrong. I sighed in relief. Nadia had saved us. Then, without a backward glance, Nadia walked out of the room with Vieru and the guards. Now that the tour was over, the guards had little interest in us. There were no reporters to talk to, and since we had been set up, no one really expected us to defect. They knew that had never been our intention.

Geza, Marta, and I went up to our rooms and grabbed our bags. We left the hotel undetected, and lost ourselves in the streets of New York City.

15.

Waiting for a Miracle

Until the last moment we were waiting for some miracle to happen. We were waiting for the nightmare to end, for things to go back to normal, for our chance to go home.

It was about 8:00 A.M. when Geza, Marta, and I walked out of our hotel and onto the streets of Manhattan. We found a small cafe and waited to see news of our defection on the television. We did not talk. We had spent the whole night discussing the pros and cons of defection; there was nothing left to say. In the early afternoon the news we had been waiting for appeared on the television.

There was Vieru and the team, at the airport, surrounded by the media. Someone tried to stick a microphone in front of Nadia's face and Vieru shoved the journalist away. Nadia and the rest of the gymnasts looked frightened and shocked. It was obvious that the whole world now knew of our defection. They moved toward their airplane and disappeared. That was all. The newscast ended and we were left alone.

Marta had an aunt named Moush who lived somewhere in New York City. We had seen her once, in 1976, at the American Cup at Madison Square Garden. She was not a close relative, just a very old Rumanian lady, Marta's father's sister. We knew she was living in Manhattan in a little bitty apartment. We had been there once, five years ago. "Let's try to find Moush," Marta suggested. We did not know on what street she lived or her telephone number.

I have always had a good sense of direction. After wandering around the city for several hours we found Moush's apartment. We went up several flights of stairs and knocked on her door. The door opened and we slowly walked inside, all the while calling out Moush's name. There was an old rocking chair in the middle of the room, and we could see from behind that someone was in the chair. Still, Moush did not answer our calls. We walked around the chair and saw that it was indeed Moush who was rocking back and forth. She was muttering, crying, and staring intently at the television in front of her.

"Moush," Marta said softly, "it's Marta and Bela . . . from Rumania . . ." While Marta tried to get her aunt's attention, I turned toward the television. What kind of show is this, I wondered, that Moush is getting so upset over. I watched the screen and there were some people shooting and diving onto the ground. The same scene kept playing over and over again. To me, it looked just like any other gangster movie. By this point Moush had recognized and welcomed us, but her eyes never left the TV. "Oh, my God, oh, my God," she said. "Uh, sit down . . . oh, my God, can you see what has happened?" Wow, this must be a great movie, I thought.

Later, after the broadcast had ended, Moush explained to us that the man who had been shot repeatedly on the screen was President Ronald Reagan. Marta, Geza, and I just looked at each other. The same thought was in all of our heads: What in the hell had we gotten ourselves into?

We spent a sleepless night on the floor of Moush's apartment. The next morning we discussed what we should do. While we did not understand English, we knew that we needed some type of certificate to allow us to stay in the country and to get a job. Two days later a friend of Moush's, a fellow defector from Rumania, took us to the Immigration Office.

We appreciated the man's help. But unfortunately, Moush's friend turned out to have a type of persecution complex. He thought there were people following him, and us. He did not try to frighten us, but he did. We were in a foreign country, without the ability to understand much of anything around us. The man thought we were surrounded by the secret police. He thought we were all going to be killed. When you come from a place where you never have peace of mind, where you are always looking over your shoulder, it's hard to break from that mind-set. That poor man was still not free.

Once at immigration, we got on line. We could not speak English, and we did not understand what forms to fill out. I looked for European faces in the line. I noticed a Russian. I asked him what the procedure was, and what forms we needed. We waited in line for hours. Around noon I reached the head of the line. I walked up to the window and looked down at a fat fellow in a chair. He was reclining, his legs up on the table. I placed my papers on the counter and looked at him expectantly. The fat man reached inside a drawer and pulled out a sandwich. He began to eat.

I smiled, tapped the counter, and pushed my papers forward. "Don't you see that I'm eating," the fat man yelled at me. I did not understand, and once again I pushed my papers forward. The man yelled at me again. I recognized his tone. And then I felt a frustration, as old as my life, well up inside of me. I began in Rumanian, "Hey, I know you. I know you. You don't know me but I know you. I grew up with you, forty years of my life. I have experienced this same situation in Rumania. You are the same goddamn lousy, lazy bureaucratic idiot that I had in my country." The man kept eating.

Later the fat man took my papers. He looked at them for a moment and then threw them back at me. What was wrong? The man pointed to all the lines I had left blank. The form was in English; the only part any of us had understood was where to put our names. "Next," the fat man yelled, and we were sent to the end of the line.

It took us the rest of the afternoon to learn from our fellow immigrants what each line meant. We completed our forms and waited on line for several more hours. When we reached the window we were sent away again. We spent more time asking questions, and by the time we learned that we were missing a form the office had closed.

The next day we returned, and finally our forms were taken. However, we didn't receive anything—not a number or card.* We did not know what to do next, so we returned to Moush's apartment. It was a time of desperation. We were like newborns. Everything we had learned in the last forty years was useless.

It was time to make plans. There were two other people in the United States who we knew. One was a Hungarian named Les who we had met during one of our tours in California. He was a teacher, and was affiliated in some way with the U.S. Gymnastics Federation. We remembered that he had said that if we were ever in California we should visit. We were grasping at straws, but Les was one of our only hopes.

Our other hope was Paul Ziert. Our relationship with Paul began before we ever personally met. I had always been amazed by Bart Conner's gymnastic ability. I always wondered, "How in the world, in America, could such a good gymnast come from such a poor

*I received a Green Card three years later, and was granted citizenship May 1, 1990.

program?" Well, Paul was Bart's coach, and because of Bart's abilities I sought out Paul. As I have said, our friendship developed over the years, from meets and tours, and was based on a mutual admiration. We called Paul "Pauli" (the Hungarian translation for Paul) and "The Happy American" because he was always smiling and laughing.

I decided to try to contact Paul. Unfortunately, I didn't know how to find him. I had no idea what city he lived in, and none of us knew how to use the telephone. I spent several frustrating hours trying to talk with operators, but none of them could understand me. I speak five languages and none of them helped!

Through Hungarian immigrants in Manhattan we continued our search for Paul. Finally a Hungarian lady located Paul in northern Oklahoma. She told us she would call him for us. Great, we thought, finally our luck was changing. The dear woman did, indeed, speak to Paul. She told him why she was calling and for whom, and that we were in New York City. When she returned to Moush's apartment to tell us that she had been successful we were ecstatic.

Paul did not call. We waited several days, but he did not contact us. We felt abandoned. What we did not know then was that our Hungarian friend had told Paul everything but where we were and how to contact us! Paul was frantic. He finally traced us through the Immigration Office and we received a call from him. Paul arranged for us to visit several cities to try to find coaching work. No one was interested in hiring me. I couldn't understand. I had been a successful Olympic gymnastics coach, but I couldn't find a coaching job. We decided that we wanted to go to California. We thought that perhaps there, in the center of the gymnastics community, we would have more luck. Paul arranged for our flight and helped us to contact Les.

When Les picked us up at the airport he told us that he had found a hotel for us to stay in for free. His friend, a Hungarian, was the assistant manager at the Beverly Wilshire Hotel, and had offered us a room for a few days. It was so ironic. There we were, no money, no prospects, not even a clean pair of socks, staying at the most exclusive hotel in Beverly Hills. At night we slept in a utility room where the hotel's cleaning personnel sometimes stayed, and during the day we rubbed shoulders with people who smelled like money.

Les tried so hard to help us. He called around to everyone he could think of, but he couldn't find us any work. "Don't worry," he would say, "I'm still working on it." I couldn't understand. I would see newspapers with our pictures in them, and I knew that our defection was getting a lot of publicity. Why wouldn't anyone hire us? I bought an English dictionary and learned a few phrases— "Hello, I am Bela Karolyi, Rumanian coach, do you have a job?" I started to look up gymnasiums in the Yellow Pages. I got some quarters and began to make calls. The refusals were prompt.

I thought that getting a job in coaching would be easy. After all, I had proven my abilities—we all had. I wasn't looking for a top position, just a secondhand coaching job. We had seen some of the gyms in California during our tours. They were huge clubs—fifteen or twenty coaches. I thought, gosh, why can't they hire their twenty-first coach?

I didn't find out until several months later why I was ostracized. It seems that negative media stories had been generated about me. The stories said that a militant Communist coach was coming to the United States, and that I was going to try to change the American system of gymnastics. I was going to bring communism to California. Bring communism? I had run for my life from communism, why would I try to bring it with me?

We ran out of time. The assistant manager at the Beverly Wilshire said we had to leave. During our stay, Geza had found a choreography job in Sacramento and when we left the hotel we parted. We knew it would be some time before we could contact each other. Marta and I did not even know where we were going, but we vowed to try. Then Marta and I asked Les to take us somewhere else to stay. Les dropped us off at a friend's house.

When I said goodbye to Les, I could tell that he felt he had failed. He said he wanted to keep trying to help, but he had done more than enough. He was a schoolteacher, and I knew he was not able to help us any longer. We thanked Les, to whom I will always be grateful, and then enjoyed the hospitality of his friend for a few days. Then, I felt it was time to take our destiny in my own hands.

Marta and I moved into a small motel in a terrible harbor area. I left Marta in the room and began walking the harbor to look for work. The streets were frightening. We were in California, and I expected to see strange creatures, but what I saw was beyond imagination. Not just sailors and poor people, not just the homeless, whores, and junkies, but really crazy people. God, it was shocking. I had never seen that part of America, I had never seen that part of society. I guess I didn't look like I fit in, because they picked on me.

I began to look for familiar facial features—from former neighboring European countries. I found someone who spoke Russian. The man I spoke with told me that I could find work at night doing manual labor, loading and unloading boats, along the docks. He told me that I would be paid $15, maybe more if I worked extra hours. That was my first job in America. Through that job I met Czechs, Poles, and Russians. They were my first friends, and they helped me find work.

I worked down at the harbor for a few weeks. Sometimes I was lucky and found work, sometimes I waited all night and got nothing. In the meantime, Marta stayed in the motel. She spent her time trying to learn English from shows like *Sesame Street*, and trying to keep the motel manager from throwing us out when we couldn't quite pay our bill.

One day my friend Milo said that he heard that nightclub owners were hiring men to clean their bars after hours. After working a night shift, I headed over to the clubs to look for a second job. Milo found a job immediately, and I continued on alone. I stopped at a saloon named To Ivan the Terrible. This place must be run by a Russian fellow, I thought, and went inside.

There was a big, fat, black-bearded guy behind the bar. "Do you speak Russian?" I asked. "What do you want?" he answered. "I am here looking for a job, do you have anything?" "You damn immigrants," he yelled, "you're coming out of the woodwork!" "Hey," I said, "I'm just looking for a job, if you don't have one I'll hit the door." "You lazy immigrant," he screamed, "I have nothing for you." I headed for the door.

"Hey," Ivan the Terrible yelled, "I'll pay you five dollars if you want to clean. You must be here at five A.M. and you have two hours to make this place spotless." I told him I'd be there the following morning. The next morning I arrived and the Russian locked me in the bar—the son of a gun locked me in! There was another man who was also there to clean—a small Asian guy. We communicated through sign language and had a good time working together. At 7:30 A.M. the Russian returned. He looked around for a few seconds and then began to cuss.

He was really screaming! He ran his finger along shelves, raved and pointed to spots that we had missed, and hurled insults in English. "Get out of here," he roared, "get out." I said, "Sure, once you pay me, I'll get out." We had been working hard for two and a half hours, and we had done as much as we could. We hadn't done a perfect job, but we had cleaned all the glasses, swept, picked up the trash . . . Finally the guy gave us each five dollars, and as we headed for the door he told us to come back at the same time tomorrow.

Every morning we went through the same charade. What a nut! But he always ended up paying us five dollars and asking us to return the next morning. One morning, after I returned to the motel,

Marta asked me how work had been. "It was all right," I answered, "I brought home forty-seven dollars, but I am working for the damndest Russian fellow now, and he screams and cusses something awful." Marta asked me what he said, and I told her that he mostly cussed in English. "What does he say?" she asked again. "Marta," I answered tiredly, "the only word I can remember is sonofabitch. Do you know what that means?"

"Let's get the dictionary," Marta suggested. She looked up "son-ofabitch" and couldn't find any such word. "Maybe it's more than one word," I suggested. Marta tried again. "Okay," she began, "here's the word *son* . . . that means the child of somebody. Now, here's the word *bitch* . . . that means a female dog. So, son of a bitch means the child of a female dog . . . a puppy!" "Hey," I said, "that guy isn't so bad. He's just calling me a little puppy—that's nice, kinda cute." The next morning I smiled every time the Russian called me a sonofabitch. I smiled, and he yelled the words louder.

In the meantime, Paul Ziert had been trying to track Marta and me down. He was running a summer gymnastics camp, and he had coaching positions for us. It took him several weeks, but finally he found us. Paul arranged for us to fly to northern Oklahoma. I was fired up. I wanted to do the best job that could humanly be done. Here was my opportunity to coach in America—there was no way I was going to mess up. There was only one problem. Paul arranged to have prepaid airline tickets waiting for us at the airport. I still did not understand much English, and when he told me how to pick up the tickets, I just said "yes, yes, yes," like I understood.

When we arrived at the airport I walked up to the first man I saw in a booth and asked for my tickets. "Excuse me, sir," I said, "my ticket to Oklahoma?" He was a man soliciting money. He laughed at me and then turned to other people to harass them for donations. Then Marta spied a sign that read "AVIS" and we immediately went over to the counter. There was a travel agency in Europe called AVIS, and we were sure we had found our tickets. After a half hour on line, we were again told that the person behind the counter didn't have our tickets.

AVIS sent me to a ticket counter. "I want my ticket to Oklahoma," I said. The ticket seller had me write down my name, and then he printed out a ticket and asked me for money. I didn't have any money, my ticket was supposed to be prepaid. Of course, we were once again at the wrong counter.

I wanted to give up. We couldn't communicate with anyone, and we couldn't find the right ticket counter because we didn't know the name of the airline. It was an impossible situation. Marta and I just stood in the middle of the airport not knowing where to turn. Then we heard a French word. We went over to a group of Frenchmen and asked them where we should go to pick up our tickets. The group's guide asked what airline, and we told him we didn't know. Bless his heart, he went to each airline and found out who had a flight going to Oklahoma at the time we were scheduled to fly. He found out we were scheduled on a Continental flight. We received our tickets and boarded a plane for Oklahoma.

Paul's gymnastics camp was having a special session when Marta and I arrived. All the big shots of the community—doctors, lawyers, community leaders—had sent their kids to the camp. Paul emphasized that Marta and I should be as nice as we could to the kids because they were the children of very important people in town.

We immediately began coaching. I still did not know English, but I tried my best to communicate with the kids. Each time they did something well I would pat them on the head and say, "Good, good, good little son of a bitch. . . . Excellent little son of a bitch."

You should have seen the eyes on those suckers. They couldn't believe their ears! Suddenly one of the kids went running to his mother—the mother went running to Paul—Paul came running over to me. "Bela," Paul said, "what exactly are you saying to the kids?" "I'm calling them good little puppies, excellent puppies—son of a bitches," I answered. "No, Bela," he explained, "son of a bitch is a bad word, not a good word." "It's not a puppy?" I asked sadly. "No, it's not a puppy," Paul answered. I was very disappointed. The only English phrase I had learned I could not use.

16.

Paul, Bart, and Bill

Paul Ziert was more than a friend to Marta and me. After we finished coaching a session of Paul's summer camp, he found assistant coaching positions for us in the physical education department of Oklahoma University. Paul also gave us coaching positions at his gymnastic club. It was more than we had ever hoped for. In addition, Bart Conner became a part of our life and a new American friend.

Six months had passed since our defection. We had gone from the streets of Manhattan, to a four-star hotel in California, to the seediest harbor in Long Beach, to Oklahoma. We knew we had been both lucky and blessed to have people who took care of us and were concerned for our welfare. We knew we were fortunate, and yet our hearts were still filled with fear and sadness. It had been six months since we had last seen our daughter, Andrea.

We could not call our daughter. We had tried, but the government had cut the phone lines to our home. We managed to communicate with a friend in Rumania, and he informed us that my old aunt was taking care of Andrea and living with her in our home. The government, however, had seized our home and taken away all our belongings except one bed. My aunt and Andrea were sharing the bed. We were destroyed with worry.

"Bela, I know a congressman in Washington, D.C., who has some involvement in the Favored Nation Status designations. Let's drive to D.C. and see if he'll meet with us," Bart Conner suggested. Favored Nation Status is a type of economic status that the United States grants to foreign countries so they can receive and sell goods to the United States without high sales taxes. It is extremely valuable to countries like Rumania. It was worth a try.

Bart and I drove to D.C. and arrived unannounced at the office of Bill Archer, Republican congressman from Texas. We spoke to his secretary and explained who we were and why we wanted to see the congressman. A few minutes later we were ushered into his office. Bart introduced me to Congressman Archer, and we told him my story. He was very concerned and immediately said he would help me.

"I am still on the committee for the Favored Nation Status for Eastern European countries—Rumania is one of those countries," Congressman Archer explained. "I can definitely try to do something about your daughter," he said. Bart spoke up, "Could you do something right away?" Congressman Archer nodded, picked up the phone, and dialed the Rumanian embassy.

"I want to speak with the ambassador," said Archer. After a short conversation, he was transferred to the ambassador's telephone line. Archer did not waste any time. "Mr. Ambassador, this is Congressman Bill Archer, what is the status of Bela and Marta Karolyi's petition for the release of their daughter from Rumania?" The ambassador's answer upset Archer. A conversation ensued of which I understood only bits. Finally, Archer said sternly into the phone. "We don't want the answer in two months, we want the answer today. Call me back today with the answer to my question . . . no, I want you to call today, not tomorrow. In fact, I will hold the line while you call your government and get me the answer." Several minutes later the ambassador came back on the line. He apologized to Archer and said that he was sorry but the man he needed to speak with was out of his office. He couldn't get an answer that day.

Bill Archer did not pause for a moment. He began, "If you do not get me an answer in twenty-four hours, I am going to personally call the Committee for Favored Nation Status and discuss Rumania's current status. We are long overdue for a discussion of this sort—there have been too many reports lately of your country's blatant disregard for civil rights." The ambassador apologized again and promised that he would try his best to get the answer as soon as possible. I pictured Marta's face when I returned home and told her I had no news of Andrea—my heart sank. We spent the rest of the afternoon in Bill Archer's office. The telephone never rang.

The answer came the next day. The release was due in three months. The congressman assured me that Andrea was fine, and that our family would soon be reunited. Three months! That meant that we would not have seen our daughter in almost a year! I thanked the congressman. He had done so much for us . . . at least we knew that Andrea was healthy. As we were about to hang up the phone, Bill Archer said, "By the way, how long have you been waiting to see Andrea?" I answered, "Six months." "*Six months—* I'm calling the embassy back right now," he said.

The next time I answered the phone, Bill Archer's first words were, "Andrea will arrive on September 18 at JFK airport in New York. Make sure you are there to pick her up." *Hallelujah!!!* Congressman Archer had cut our wait from three months to a matter of weeks. Bill Archer also got the telephone restrictions lifted from our home, and we were able to talk to our daughter and my aunt.

They told us that they had been under house arrest for all those months. The police had severely restricted their visitors and activities, and had followed them wherever they went.

In preparing for Andrea's arrival, Marta and I took what little money we had earned and bought bedroom furniture for her. Marta made curtains for her room, and for her tiny canopy bed. And we tried to decorate her mirror and walls with bright happy pictures.

On September 18 we stood behind a glass panel and anxiously scanned the faces of the passengers disembarking from our daughter's flight. I will never forget the feeling, watching people come out of the doorway and waiting to see Andrea. Finally we saw an old woman come out, and she was holding the hand of a child. We couldn't see the face of the child because of all the people in the way. Then Marta just started screaming, "Andrea, Andrea, Andrea!" Suddenly the child turned her little smiling face toward us and yelled, "Mommy, Mommy!"

Marta went racing past the customs officials and the two flew into each other's arms. They were just crying and crying. The customs people were very nice about it, but they made me wait outside the gates. Marta had completely forgotten about me! She and Andrea went through customs together and got our daughter's little suitcase. Finally they came out and I held us all together in one big hug.

We returned to Oklahoma, and to the task of getting Andrea ready for her next big ordeal—school. Can you imagine, a little girl who has been separated from her parents for six months comes to a strange country where she can understand no one, and has to enter a new school, meet new friends, and learn a new language? It was overwhelming.

On her first day of school, Marta and I took Andrea to the principal and met with her teachers. We explained that she did not know English, and that if they could help her get adjusted we would really appreciate it. The principal and teachers were nice, but it was a public school and they just didn't have the time to really help Andrea. Of course, they didn't say that, but it quickly became clear.

Andrea never complained. Every day we picked her up from the school yard where she stood alone. We asked her how her day had been and she always said fine. We noticed that she was becoming very quiet and sad. One night Marta went into her room to tuck her in for the night, and Andrea said, "Mommy, nobody's talking to me." Marta tried to explain that the kids didn't talk to her because they didn't know her language, not because they didn't like her. It didn't matter. Andrea was so sad that we thought she might get sick.

There was a private Baptist school in Oklahoma. The principal of the school had come to me to ask if I would teach some gymnastics classes. I agreed to teach if I could send Andrea to his school, and if he would assign someone to help her socialize with the kids and learn English. He agreed. He told us that the school already had several Korean kids who were adjusting wonderfully to their new country and to English. Marta and I were thrilled.

It was worse than the public school. No care for Andrea whatsoever. Her classes were filled with kids of all ages and all levels of learning. Andrea was neglected—it was a mess. Marta bought English guides and conversation manuals and tried to teach Andrea herself, but she didn't know enough English yet to teach her. We were worried and upset about our daughter, and we couldn't seem to find a solution.

Several weeks later we were picking Andrea up from school when we noticed that she was finally talking to other children. It was then that we realized that the best teachers were the children. Even though no one took special care of Andrea, she had learned by listening, and had finally found the courage to test out her new language skills. I asked her, "How are you talking to those kids? Are you talking Rumanian or Hungarian?" She didn't know that she was speaking English, she just said, "I'm talking like everybody else." "You mean," I continued, "they ask questions and you answer, and you ask questions and they answer?" Andrea said that was exactly right.

It was a beautiful thing, watching our daughter talk to a bunch of children. We listened to her voice and there wasn't even an accent. She was becoming fluent in English. We planned to return Andrea to public school—we were confident that she would now do well. However, we never got the opportunity, because we left Oklahoma in December and moved to Houston, Texas.

17.

Texas-Time

In December 1982, I was approached by two men from Houston, Texas—Patrick Alexander and Mike Roland. Alexander was a gymnastics coach and Roland was a businessman. They told me that they planned to turn an existing gymnastics facility into a world-class training center, and they wanted me to be a partner in their venture.

Alexander and Roland flew Marta and me to Houston, and we toured several gymnasiums. We assumed that the two men owned these facilities, and we were extremely excited by what we were seeing. The men also mentioned that they were in negotiations to purchase another gymnasium. Ultimately, that gymnasium would be the central facility that they had described to us. Marta and I assumed that in the meantime we would operate out of the other gymnasiums that we had toured. Unfortunately, the facilities they had shown us were not their own.

I do not think that Roland and Alexander maliciously lured me to Houston. They wanted to make their deal look attractive, and they truly planned to turn the gymnasium they were negotiating for, once they had secured the deal, into a gymnastics center. But things did not go as planned.

Marta and I packed up our belongings and moved to Houston with our daughter. We soon realized that there was no available facility. It took several weeks before a third associate, a banker from Cleveland, Texas, named Kerry Gedder, was brought into the deal. Kerry provided some of the money needed to finance the project, and by February the negotiations to lease the facility and buy the business were completed.

Things did not go well: The facility that the partners had leased was pretty isolated. There simply weren't enough clients (kids). The gymnasium was very simple and basic—nothing that would have created a special impression on children or their families. We did our best, but we had only a few gymnasts. Things began to fall apart.

A few months later Pat Alexander came to me. "Bela," he said, "I'm afraid we are going to have to give up the project." "Good Lord," I said, "we are going to have to hit the road again." Pat told me that there was another possibility. "If you want to keep trying to make the gymnasium a success, you can take over the lease and pay the partners off," he explained. Pay the partners off? Their original investment was $40,000. I would have to pay each partner $10,000! There was absolutely no way I could do that.

I turned to Kerry Gedder. We had become good friends over the months—he had a wife and young child, and Marta, Andrea, and I had spent time with them. I asked him what I should do. "Bela," Kerry said, "don't worry about paying the partners off. If you want to stay, then stay." "I cannot stay, I have no money," I said. "I'll find a way for you to cover your responsibilities to the partners for as long as possible," Kerry explained. "Your obligation is to pay the rent, expenses, and utilities, and to find a way to eventually pay back the partners and buy the facility from the owner. When you have the money you can pay me back."

Kerry arranged for me to get a low-interest loan from his bank. Slowly I paid back the partners for their investment in the gym. I had managed to pay off the partners, but now the question was how were we going to manage to stay in the facility? We had only a few gymnasts, not enough to pay even the electric bills. We couldn't afford our utility bill, let alone our lease payments.

I was desperate. I went to every bank in the area to borrow money. No one had any trust in me. The first question I was asked was, what is your credit record? Credit record? I didn't even own a credit card. The second question was: How much money does your business generate? I was stupid and honest—I told them the truth. Then they asked how many gymnasts we had and how much each gymnast paid us. The interviews always ended the same way: "We're very sorry, we'd really like to help you, but there is absolutely no way our board of directors would ever okay a loan for you."

We gave up. Bill collectors began to come around and ask for the rent, the utilities . . . I had no money to pay them. Then our good friend Patrick Alexander stepped back in, as he had several times in the past. He arranged for me to have a position in the physical education department at Sam Houston State University. He also found a home for us to live in, and arranged, through the college, to get an unbelievably low mortgage on the house. Marta and I got a second wind. We agreed that we would try once again to make ends meet. We would struggle to pay what had to be paid. If the day came where we could not pay and we were kicked out of our home or the gymnasium in Houston, then we would be kicked out. No matter what, we would do as much as we could to survive.

If we were to survive, we desperately needed to expand our client base at the gymnasium. I had no money for advertising, so Marta and I made handwritten flyers and placed them on doors and car windshields. Then I turned my eyes on the gym. It was really basic, and we did not have the money to fix it up. I did what I could. I cleaned the gym from floor to ceiling. Then I went to some banks in town and collected free posters. They weren't gymnastics posters, but I put them all over the walls to add some color.

In a short time the number of gymnasts at our facility tripled. The kids were the best advertisements we could have hoped for. They told all their classmates how they were doing gymnastics in the afternoons with a famous coach, and how much fun they were having with Marta and me. We had about 100 students, generating enough income to pay our utility bill. A few weeks later we expanded to 200 gymnasts, and we paid off our bills, including our back payments. I was just beginning to think that we could survive and thrive when our landlord paid a visit.

Our monthly rent was approximately $4,000. We did not have the money. "How much can you pay?" asked our landlord. "I have $400 to put toward the rent this month. But we are starting to do well here . . . please give us a chance," I said. The landlord had no other offer for the space, so he agreed to take our money and allow us to stay. The next month we expanded to 250 gymnasts and were able to pay $3,000 rent. By the summer of 1982 we had more than three hundred gymnasts. It was then that we met Larry Parker.

Larry Parker was a banker with the Texas Commerce Bank whom I went to see about a loan to purchase the gymnasium from its owner. I was tired of always wondering when the floor would be pulled out from under us. I knew that we were always in danger of being kicked out by the owner. There was always a chance that he would find a tenant willing to pay more for our gymnasium. Larry came down to the gym and looked around. He promised me that he would call and let me know if a loan was possible.

We were informed soon after Larry's visit that we would receive our loan. Larry Parker had filed all our paperwork and applications, and he had personally guaranteed our loan to the bank and the board of directors. He is a great man—we will be grateful to him for the rest of our lives. In August 1982 we became our own landlord, and the building was put in our name. From that moment on we stood on our own two feet.

After that things happened very fast. In 1981, I had received a call from a mother in Gary, Indiana. She had told me that her dream was to have Bela Karolyi coach her daughter. I remember speaking with Paul Ziert about what I should do. Paul said, "Bela, this is your first inquiry in the United States, it will be hard to turn down. . . ."

I desperately wanted to train the woman's daughter, but at the time I did not feel that I had anything to offer her. I was not running my own intensive program, and the child would not receive the best training possible. She would not receive my best. I also didn't want to mislead the mother. I asked her to please be patient, and that when I had a better position and an appropriate facility I would call her. She told me she understood, but that she would be waiting anxiously. I called the woman in August 1982. Several weeks later I met her daughter—Diane Durham.

18.

Words

One sunny afternoon in Houston, Texas, I picked up my daughter, Andrea, from school. She was excited because her teacher had given her a special homework assignment that Mommy and Daddy could help her with. "Daddy," she said, "I need to do a New Year's resolution." I went crazy.

"No revolution, no revolution in my home," I yelled. "Absolutely not, period." Andrea was silent as we pulled into the driveway of our home. "Absolutely no revolution," I muttered as I slammed the car door and stalked into the house. What kind of school was I sending my daughter to, that her teacher would try to disrupt my house, my family?

Later in the evening Marta came into the den. "Bela," she said, "Andrea is upset because you won't help her with her homework." "Marta, her teacher wants us to help her start a revolution, I won't be a part of that, and she won't either!" "Bela, it's a New Year's *resolution,* not *revolution,*" Marta said. I did not know the differ-ence. "It means making a positive goal for the New Year, like not eating too much ice cream or being nice to people," Marta explained.

Old ways of thinking die hard.

19.

Power Packs

I have always been a fighter. When I arrived in the United States I fought my own fears. I fought to find work, to learn English, and to carve a niche for myself and my family in our new country. When I had finally purchased my first gymnasium, I thought the fighting was over. But I was naive. I did not realize that one of the greatest fights of my life was yet to come.

"American gymnasts cannot ever successfully compete against the Soviets or the Rumanians. American gymnasts have too good a life to accept the harsh preparation needed to create highly competitive performances. American kids are spoiled and lazy; they only want to have fun. If you push them too hard, American gymnasts will give up." In the early 1980s, this was the type of information that the coaches of the U.S. National Team were feeding the media in an effort to cover their own inadequacies. I remember the American team's pitiful performance in front of their own supporters at the 1979 World Championships in Fort Worth, Texas. If I was a National team coach, I would have been embarrassed, too. The strange thing was that the coaching was never at fault. It was always the lazy kids.

Kids, whether Rumanian, Russian, or American, are kids. If they are talented and receive proper coaching and positive encouragement, they will fight to improve—they will fight to win. Not only did American coaches have excuses for their gymnasts' inability to excel, they had excuses for why gymnasts should not turn to Karolyi for coaching. There were many public statements made about my lack of experience in working with American kids. Crazy statements aimed at undermining my reputation.

I was naive at the time. I did not know that American coaches had given up on the possibility of being internationally competitive. All I knew was that a little girl from Gary, Indiana, was coming to me for coaching. Diane Durham would get the best I could give her—my kind of coaching. I didn't care whether I was in Rumania or the United States, to me there was only one way to prepare for competition—intensively.

I did not realize that Diane and I were about to challenge the U.S. system of gymnastics in two profound ways. First, we were about to prove that American gymnasts could successfully compete nationally and internationally. Second, we were about to prove that black gymnasts, who had never before been thought of as having the body constitution and temperament necessary for artistic and mellow performances, could excel in gymnastics at every level.

When I think back, I realize the importance of Diane Durham's contribution to the whole turnaround of American gymnastics. This little black kid, who nobody had paid attention to, turned the entire American gymnastics community upside-down.

When Diane arrived at my gym, I placed her in a "normal" pattern of instruction—physical conditioning and hours of intensive practice. She improved unbelievably. We had the greatest time watching her unique power and energy. Diane was an extremely aggressive competitor, she was tough, strong, and powerful. We organized a team of local gymnasts around Diane, and took them to the Junior National Championships. Diane won the elite division. She was thirteen years old at the time.

Around the same time, I became aware of a promising young gymnast, who I noticed performing at a USGF competition. She was a little bundle of energy—all smiles. She wasn't the most successful child at the competition, but that's never what I look for. I look for kids with an attitude. I look for the ones who are not the strongest or fastest, but who are excited and jump and push to get that quarter of an inch ahead of everyone else.

As a coach, I never look for the super-talented child. Usually that type of child doesn't have the patience or the desire to work hard enough or long enough for results. Super-talented kids can easily accomplish what other kids have to work hard for, so they think everything should be easy, and if it isn't they have no patience to work to raise their abilities to a higher level. Mary Lou Retton wasn't a fantastic talent when I first watched her perform, but I could tell she had the drive and desire to be better than the rest.

We spent the next six months preparing both Diane and Mary Lou for the U.S. Senior National Championships. This would be our true testing ground—the first time that our gym competed in the U.S. Senior Nationals, and the first time that our gymnasts would have the opportunity to make an impression on the American gymnastics community.

Working with Diane and Mary Lou was a new experience for Marta and me. Diane was a stubborn, strong, sturdy, and truly honest kid. She never lied to us or played games. Mary Lou's personality matched well with Diane's. She was another open person, but more sensitive than Diane. Mary Lou had more ups and downs. When we first started to work she had mood changes fifteen times a day—crying, laughing, happy, sad—she was something else. What I loved most about those two was that they always told us what was on their minds. We had never experienced that before.

Because the government was always hanging over their heads, Rumanian kids were under constant pressure to keep their feelings to themselves. A ferocious type of pressure. They could have been eliminated at any moment if they did not meet specific criteria. They were frightened of the system, of the coaching, and of responding in any way to their emotions. Diane and Mary Lou were open books.

In the beginning, I was a bit worried about one aspect of Mary Lou's personality. She was so easygoing in practice. She didn't seem too concerned about the final product of her performance, and I thought that she might be careless in competitions. I was wrong. Mary Lou was one of the most ambitious gymnasts I have ever worked with. It was just that she had such a damn good disposition. She was always ready to joke, ready to love. You could not be sleepy around her.

Mary Lou was the sunshine of Marta's and my career. Years after 1984, when Mary Lou was asked about her success, she said that she always listened to me 100 percent—she figured that if I made Nadia, I had to be right about everything. It was a child's mentality, but that type of belief and confidence in herself and in me helped her tremendously and made her a joy to coach.

In 1983, Diane swept the Senior Nationals. Mary Lou tied for third. We did not know then that Diane was the first African-American in the history of U.S. gymnastics to win a Senior National title. We were used to winning—everywhere we had ever competed in the past, we had won. Nothing seemed unusual to us. Nothing, except that not one coach from the women's gymnastic community came over to shake our hands.

Diane and Mary Lou had shown a style and technical ability that had never been seen before in American gymnasts. Diane, who nobody ever considered having a favorable body type for gymnastics, had become the national champion. She had, in one competition, shown that American gymnasts could perform on a superior level. I had introduced a powerful new style of gymnastics to the American community, which was more proper and accessible for American kids in general, yet nobody recognized this fact. And nobody came over to talk with me, to congratulate me, or to welcome me to U.S. gymnastics.

The media jumped into the situation with both feet. "Now wait a second, wait a second," the media began to write. "Maybe, with a coach like Karolyi, the U.S. *can* be internationally competitive in gymnastics. Maybe the problem all these years has been the coaching, not the abilities of the gymnasts." This type of media attention angered a lot of American coaches.

The coaches fought back. I will never forget the derogatory statements they made about Mary Lou and Diane. They attacked their style, abilities, and appearance. It was so hurtful to the kids. One American coach said that the kids "looked like fireplugs on the corner of a street in Chicago." It was true that my kids were stockier and more physically powerful than the typical American gymnast, who was modeled after those of Rumania, the U.S.S.R., and Germany. But I wasn't trying to re-create an old phenomenon, I wanted a new one.

I have always known that the only way to win is to introduce something new, something sensational. To win you must break with the system—go the opposite way. Copying can only make you second-best. The Soviets and Rumanians had become smaller and smaller, almost airy, like butterflies winging around. They no longer presented physical power and technical ability. American gymnasts had copied that in an effort to be internationally competitive. I knew that we had to create a different style and body type—not just to be competitive, but to win. Diane and Mary Lou were well built and possessed great power and explosiveness. They were everything that the world of gymnastics had moved away from.

That's it, I thought, they are the new style. They are the future of gymnastics.

At first it was ridiculous how the kids were underscored. The appreciation was so lacking . . . but we didn't get depressed. "That's just part of the fight," I told Diane and Mary Lou. "Let's go for it!" And after the Nationals, no matter what anyone said, we had proven what we had set out to prove: American gymnasts could be champions if they were trained right. They had the drive, the spirit, and the talent.

That year the pre-Olympic competitions were held at the Pauley Pavilion in Los Angeles. I have always said that the pre-Game events are the most important gymnastics competition in the world, save the Olympics. Everyone is there—Soviets, Rumanians, everyone. Historically, what happens at the pre-Olympics will most probably happen at the Olympics.

It was at the pre-Olympic Games that Diane Durham's true contribution to the world of gymnastics was made. She was the one who set the stage. She was the one who pulled American gymnastics out of sweet mediocrity and showed that with dedicated practice and strong, aggressive performances, Americans could be as good as the Soviets and Rumanians. In fact, Diane showed that Americans could even be better. Diane placed American gymnastics at the point where we were finally considered an international power.

Diane took first place all-around in the pre-Games competition, and Mary Lou placed an impressive second. For me, that was a strong enough statement to my critics, "Yes, we are ready to be recognized, and we demand appreciation from both our own country and from abroad." There was no longer any doubt as to Diane's or Mary Lou's talent. There was no longer any doubt about whether the color of Diane's skin or either kid's body type would negatively affect their performances. And there was no longer any question as to whether Bela Karolyi could successfully coach American gymnasts.

Just as negative publicity draws countless critics, positive public-ity draws countless piranhas. After the pre-Olympic Games, we returned to the gym to prepare Diane and Mary Lou for the Senior National Competition and the Olympic Trials. Soon after our re-turn, a man named Scott Crouse also flew to Houston. He met with Diane Durham and her parents, and persuaded Diane to leave our gym.

Scott Crouse was the former technical director for the U.S. Gymnastics Federation. He is a man who considers himself the greatest technical gymnastics specialist in the country. When we arrived in the United States he was just as frightened as all the other coaches. He came out and heavily criticized everything I was doing, and actively discouraged gymnasts from coming to my gym for training. But that was before we were successful.

When we returned to Houston he met with Diane's parents. According to the Durhams, he told them that the Karolyis were favoring Mary Lou. That Diane, because she was black and Mary Lou was white, was not getting enough attention. The Karolyis, he said, have no experience in working with black people, and that will negatively affect Diane. He said that the best way to get Diane the exposure and training she needed was to move her to his gym.

I did not know what Scott Crouse was planning. I did not even know that he was meeting with the Durhams. I only know that in our gymnasium we have never made concessions for anyone. It didn't matter whether Diane was the pre-Olympic champion or not. She was treated the same as Mary Lou, and she was expected to behave herself and train just as professionally as the other gymnasts. Diane and her parents made a decision without consulting me. One day they were just gone.

It was a hard situation. I was sad that the Durhams hadn't even talked with me, but I understood. When a child becomes a personal-ity in gymnastics they are very vulnerable. Vulnerable, because the parents become nervous and suspicious. They begin to wonder, is their daughter the best. Is she getting the best training and the most attention? Then they start to listen to the people around them. And unfortunately, some of those people are less than honest, as well as bad advisers.

If you really want to do great damage to a child gymnast, just pick up the phone and call her parents. Say things like, "Well, I must tell you that your daughter is the most wonderful gymnast I have ever seen. How many medals do you think she'll get in the Olympics? Only five? No, she's so fantastic she'll probably get seven or eight golds! But, really, I must tell you that she isn't getting a lot of attention from her coach. I see him looking the other way. . . . Maybe it's because she's black, or short, or blonde . . ." Parents are so vulnerable that they'll believe just about anything.

So Diane was gone. We began to train for the Senior Nationals. Mary Lou was improving by leaps and bounds. Then I received a call from Paul Ziert. "Bela," he said, "there is a little girl, a sweet girl from California, who quit gymnastics some time ago but is considering coming back if you are willing to coach her. This is her last chance, so her parents came to me and asked if I'd talk with you." "I don't know, Paul," I said, "you know her better than I do. I have no idea if she can come back or not. Is she in good physical shape?" Paul told me to give her a chance. What the hell, we had a spot open.

When Julianne McNamara arrived at our gym in 1984 she was out of shape. In training, she dragged her little feet around the floor—she could barely move because of her sore muscles. Bless her heart, I've never seen someone so tired. But Julianne was tenacious. She was a lovely young girl, very airy and skinny. She could swing on the bars beautifully—I mean, God made her for swinging on the bars. It was a delight to watch her and spot and teach her. Several months later, just in time for the Senior National Championships, Julianne was back in competitive shape.

Mary Lou swept the National Championships. Julianne placed

second all around. Several other gymnasts from our club also placed in the top five. Diane Durham finished seventh in the Nationals. We had not seen Diane for several months and I was shocked at her deterioration.

That evening we had a celebration dinner. I toasted the kids, "I'm proud of you—you all really went for it! From now on we are going to grab the bull by the horns and go forward to the Olympics." We were all in a happy mood as we entered the lobby of our hotel. I saw Diane's mom, dad, and sister sitting in the lobby. Mrs. Durham walked over to me. "Bela," she began, "I want to tell you that what happened was dead wrong. You were the only people who sincerely appreciated us and treated us as friends. I don't know why we took Diane to Scott Crouse, I just can't find an explanation. I don't know why we did it, but I want to ask if Diane can come back." I said, "You know very well that our doors are always open to you. We've never had an argument, you guys left without talking to us. Sure, the door is open whenever you want to return."

Diane returned immediately. Unfortunately, we only had a few months before the Olympic Trials. Diane had lost much of her conditioning and had some injuries. However, we went into the final stage of preparation with high intensity. Diane was frustrated, but she pushed and pulled and worked. It was unbelievable how strong she got in so short a time. Her explosive power returned and she made up the distance.

By the time the Olympic Trials came around, the three—Mary Lou, Julianne, and Diane—were a power pack. It was exciting to imagine just what kind of sweep they would accomplish in the Olympics. We went into the trials feeling strong, knowing that we would dominate the scene. Mary Lou had developed her powerful consistent and aggressive style, Julianne was smooth and graceful, and Diane was a tornado, passionate and exciting to watch.

After the compulsories we placed first, second, and third (Mary Lou, Julianne, and Diane). Diane's strength was always the optionals, that's where she excelled, where her unbelievable physical strength and style impressed everyone. We began the optionals and Diane immediately moved up. Then came her third event—vault.

Diane executed her first vault. It wasn't a good one. Her arm slipped off the horse and she ended up with a short landing. It wasn't a failed vault, but she only received a 9.45. When Diane landed she sprained her ankle. It was not a major sprain. Not a tear of ligaments or a dislocation or break, just an ordinary sprain. In gymnastics, sprains are not dramatic or competition breaking accidents. I decided that Diane's first score was good enough to maintain a high position.

I told Diane not to do her second vault. "Put some ice on it," I said, "and let's get a bandage. Your next, and last, event is the bars, so don't worry." "How am I going to perform with my ankle?" she asked. I said, "Diane, it's the bars, you won't be on your ankle. Keep your routine the same, just do a simple dismount. Be prepared to perform in a few minutes," I advised. Then I ran off to spot Mary Lou's double layout on the floor and Julianne's dismount from the beam.

I had five gymnasts in that Olympic Trial. Each needed different protection and they all performed within minutes of each other. I had to run from event to event to spot each one. From across the floor I saw that Diane had a crowd of people around her. I didn't like that. I was running to help everyone, and I couldn't get to her right away. When I finally ran over to Diane, she was surrounded by coaches and trainers.

Cheryl Grace, an assistant to the president of the Gymnastics Federation (Mike Jacki), was talking to Diane. "Diane," she said, "you don't have to continue to compete. I don't want to see you aggravate your injury . . ." "Diane," I said, "you are on the bars soon, get your hand grips on." "I can't," she began, "my ankle really hurts . . ." "Diane," I barked, "get over to the goddamn bars." She put her grips on and moved toward the bars.

If I have learned anything throughout the years, it's that it's not over till it's over. You never assume that your place is guaranteed in any competition, and you never give up a performance unless it is unavoidable.

I watched Diane chalk up. It was almost time for her bar routine. I ran to spot Mary Lou on the vault, and then raced back to the bars to help Diane perform. There was someone else on the bars. "Marta," I yelled, "did Diane already perform?" Marta said that she had not yet performed. I turned and saw Diane sitting on the bench. "Diane, what are you doing? Didn't I tell you to get ready for the bars," I said. "Yes," she answered, "but I'm skipping the event. They told me I could skip the event because of my ankle." Skipping the event? I said, "Diane, you are wrong, you are wrong. The competition is not over yet . . . it's not over till it's over."

I stormed over to the jury and demanded that Diane be given the chance to compete on the bars. They told me her time was over and she was scratched. She had willingly scratched herself, they said. Then they told me not to worry, that Diane was on the Olympic team and everything would be fine.

The competition ended. Mary Lou and Julianne took first and second. Diane placed ninth. It took less than fifteen minutes for the judges to announce the Olympic team. During that time Don Peters, the National and Olympic team coach, raced over to the judges waving the rules and regulations of the U.S. Olympic Committee (U.S.O.C.). The rules stated that no athlete could qualify for the Olympic team without finishing the competition. Since Diane had scratched herself from the bars, she was automatically eliminated from the Olympic team.

Don Peters had watched Diane scratch herself knowing that by doing so she would be eliminated. He just let it happen, quiet like a fish. And with the elimination of Diane, a space was opened for one of his club's gymnasts.

I fought fiercely. "It was the fault of everyone here and of the Federation that Diane scratched herself from the bars," I said. "She was told that her place was guaranteed, and we must all take responsibility and open the way for this young athlete to compete in the Olympics." No one listened. No one defended Diane's rights. I appealed to the U.S.O.C., I pleaded with them, but no one spoke for Diane.

It was like fighting windmills. I realized then that we were hitting the same damn stone wall, we were fighting the same bureaucracy we had fought in Rumania. An administration that wanted total control and domination and was afraid of any individual becoming too powerful.

It was a heartbreaking moment—for Diane, her family, Marta and me, for everyone. In my life I have never been so hurt or frustrated. My mind could not accept what was happening. I had accepted injustice all of my life, but injustice aimed at a child was too much. Through the years, even the most horrible situations get easier to deal with, get rosier and less painful, but not that one. That one is a wound that will never heal. I blame the Federation, the U.S.O.C., and myself. Regardless of whether or not I could have done something, I will always share a certain portion of the responsibility.

I do not think that Cheryl Grace acted viciously. I think that her intention was not to eliminate Diane. She acted according to some rule of decency, with consideration for Diane's welfare. She wanted to protect a young athlete from injury in an effort to save her talent for the Olympic Games. However, I do not say the same for Don Peters. He eliminated a tremendously talented American athlete from the Olympic Games. By citing an unknown rule, he had Diane Durham eliminated. Everyone at the competition had expected Diane to be a member of the Olympic team. She was one of our best hopes for the gold. Don Peters was the Olympic coach; he should have worked to produce the best possible team for his country.

When we left for the Olympic Games, Diane Durham ended her gymnastics career.

20.

Parents

After the Olympic Trials I saw my parents for the first time since my defection. It was the first time in their lives that my mother and father had been to the United States. Marta, Andrea, and I picked them up at the airport and brought them to our home in Houston. We sat for several hours and tried to fill in the missing years.

My parents' reaction to our life in America, and our success, was interesting. There is a false picture that most European people have about the United States and the living standards. Most Europeans think that everyone in America has a big house and lots of money. They don't even question how you get things, they just assume that the government gives you everything. That was the mentality my parents had when they visited. They couldn't recognize the hardships that Marta and I went through to get where we were.

The morning after my parents arrived, Marta and I had to go to the gym. We hadn't yet reached the point where we had anyone else working for us—we were the office personnel, the coaches for every age group, and the janitors. We left my parents at home with instructions to wait for us to return. We told them they could walk around the yard, watch television, listen to music and eat, or make any type of food they wanted.

At 9:30 A.M. I got a call from my neighbor. "Bela, do you have guests at your house?" I told my neighbor that my parents were visiting. "Well, your parents just took off and they are walking right down the middle of the road in the direction of the four-lane highway." Oh, my gosh! I raced out of the gym and into my car to find my parents. They didn't speak any English; they didn't know their way around—holy cow!

When I spotted them, my father was walking proudly with my mother on his arm. He was tipping his hat to all the cars that were driving on lawns to pass them. In five more minutes he would have reached Highway 1960. "Dad, what are you doing?" I asked. "Oh, Bela," said my father, "we are just going shopping." Shopping? "Dad, you have no money." "Sure I have money, Bela," my dad interrupted. "Your money is no good here, Dad," I explained. My father told me not to worry, he'd just have the store owner write up a bill. I tried to explain that supermarkets here weren't like those at home. Finally I got my parents into the car.

I asked my father why he and Mom were walking down the middle of the road. "Bela," he said, "this is a beautiful walkway, it isn't a road." My father thought that everything in America was supposed to be bigger than anywhere else. He thought that included the sidewalks. "Daddy, this is a road, that's why people are driving on it and not walking—there is no walkway." He couldn't understand how people could shop without a walkway. "That's why they're driving," I explained. Even after I explained, I could tell that my father didn't really believe me.

I took them to the grocery store. They weren't too impressed with the big selection. All they saw were the vegetables and spices that were missing. I drove my parents around Houston and then dropped them at home before I went back to the gym. I had a strange feeling that they were going to take off again. "Dad," I said, "please don't leave again, don't take off." My father said, "No worries."

I went home at noon to check on them. The doors were wide open, just like back home in Rumania. I checked the streets, the entire subdivision—I couldn't find them. Finally I spotted them— they were about a hundred yards from Highway 1960. They were standing in the yard of an old woman who was working in her garden. My father was telling her, in Hungarian, his life story. He was telling her about his visit, about the plane ride, the airport, the grocery store, our house, and his son, Bela, when I arrived. The poor old lady just stared at Dad while he babbled. When we left, my father whispered that the woman had been very rude, she hadn't said one word.

That night I tried to establish some ground rules. I told my parents that they had to stay on our property. If they left the house, they had to shut the doors. I told them there were no walkways, so they had to stay around our home. My father told me that was fine, he'd visit the park by our house. There was no park. My father said, "What do you call all the green grass around your house?" "Daddy," I said, "those are other people's lawns, it's private property." "Fine," my father responded, "I'll just go in the park behind their houses." I explained that backyards were also private property. You must stay in our front and backyard, I told him.

The next morning my father was up at the crack of dawn. He stood in our front yard and greeted everyone who walked or drove by. When he came in for breakfast he told me that everyone in America was rude. No one even returned his greeting. "Daddy," I said, "they don't understand you, just don't bother them." "But I am using sign language," he said. My father was in the army, and when he was captured and imprisoned during World War I he talked with Russian people by using sign language.

A few quiet days passed. My father and mother were content with walking around our yard. Content until my father spied the sweet Spanish woman who lived across the street. My father began to talk to her in a combination of French, German, and Hungarian—it was really something. The woman was a housewife, so she was home during the day, and my father began to sit with her each day and tell her stories about himself and his family. They actually communicated fairly well, and my father thought she was the dearest woman in the world.

My parents had visited for four days when my mother told me that she and Dad were planning to leave the next morning. They were supposed to stay for several months. "Why do you want to leave, Mom?" I asked. "Well," she said, "the chickens are at home and the dog and cat, and who is going to feed them?" My sister lived in my parents' home, and she was taking care of the house and the animals. "Mom," I said, "don't worry about the damn chickens. If the chickens die I will buy you a thousand more chickens." But she had made up her mind. "Bela, we've had a great time, but we are ready to go home. Dad misses his bed, and we are worried about what might happen if we get sick over here," she explained. "Mom, if you get sick we have doctors." "Bela, we're going home," my mother said.

Before my parents returned home, I did get the chance to talk to my father about the past—a subject we had always avoided. My father told me that he had been angry with me for choosing physical education and not going into engineering. Then he said that even though he hadn't approved, he was glad now that I had made my own choice.

Somewhere deep in my heart I knew all those years that my father was proud of me. But he had never shown it. He had never come out and said, "Good job, son. I'm proud of you." No matter how old you get, you always want to hear those words from your father. He never said those exact words to me, but during that visit he finally let me know that that was how he felt. "I'm glad you made your own choice" wasn't quite the same as "I'm proud of you," but it was close enough.

21.

Boycott Busters

I n 1980, the Americans and others boycotted the Olympics because of the Russian invasion of Afghanistan. I remember thinking how crazy the Americans were to willingly choose not to defend their position of power in the world of athletics. To anyone immersed in a Communist or Socialist system, athletics were a country's most powerful propaganda tool. To relinquish that tool was senseless. The 1980 Games went forward full-tilt. No one even mentioned the teams that were not there. And those athletes who had trained their whole lives for that magic moment when they competed in the Olympics were left with their dreams shattered.

In 1984, the Soviets and East Germans turned around and boycotted the Olympics in America. Their reasoning was that they had to protect the honor, dignity, and life of their athletes who might be the objects of political and criminal attacks by extremist groups in Los Angeles. Their real motive was revenge for 1980. Most of the Warsaw Pact nations followed suit. Once again, the only ones who were hurt were the athletes.

Rumania decided to enter the 1984 Olympic Games for two reasons. First, Nicolae Ceauşescu knew that Rumania's participation in the '84 Games would be a public relations coup for his country. Rumania had a very controversial human rights track record. That record was what the U.S. government evaluated before granting Favored Nation Status, and that status was economically vital for Rumania. So Rumania became the "boycott buster." Rumanians walked into the Olympic Games with their heads held high— look at us, they said, we are here to participate in the Games and support the United States. We are heroes. Ceauşescu was favored by the U.S. government for his actions.

The second reason for the president of Rumania to send his athletes to Los Angeles was his son, Nicu. Nicu was the delegation leader for the '84 Games. His father sent him specifically to be introduced to the rest of the world as a hero, a friend, and an ally. Ceauşescu was grooming the dark prince to be his successor. Nadia was also part of the delegation. With Nadia, Nicu achieved tremendous positive propaganda for his country and for himself.

I was thrilled at Rumania's decision. Their participation would give the gymnastic competition a new dimension. Rumania had maintained a leading position in the world of gymnastics and came into 1984 as World Champions. That meant that the fight and the athletic spectacle would be just as high as if everyone else was there. That was important to me.

It was also important to me to have the opportunity to see the Rumanian team once again. Most of the kids on the team were my former students. Among them was little Ecaterina (Kati) Szabo. Kati had started out as a little bug. She was only five years old when she began training with us. She grew up and became European Champion under our tutelage. In 1983, Kati won the World Championship in floor exercise, and her gymnastic value and capability were incredible. Her style and Mary Lou's were very similar—all power. I knew that the '84 Olympics would not only be spectacular but would break a tradition. The butterflies would finally be forever wiped out of gymnastics. A new style, power gymnastics, would become an international reality.

In 1984, I had two gymnasts competing in the Olympics—Mary Lou Retton and Julianne McNamara. Two athletes who needed my attention, coaching, and physical and emotional support. But Don Peters, the 1984 Olympic team coach, refused to let me into the arena or onto the arena floor to coach my gymnasts. It was as if he did not want anyone to challenge him, or to have more visibility than he did.

I turned to Mike Jacki, the head of the U.S. Gymnastics Federation. Mike was formerly associated with the AMF Corporation—the manufacturers of the gymnastics equipment used in the Games. I asked him whether it would be possible to get a pass into the gymnasium as an equipment handler. Mike talked to Larry Fie, the head of AMF's Equipment Division, and together they agreed to give me a pass that would allow me into the Pavilion but not onto the floor.

At least I'll be near my kids, I thought, as I entered the arena for the first day of the competition. However, as I stepped into the arena I was apprehended by the organizers of the Games. They said that my pass wasn't good for the competition, only for the setup of equipment prior to the Games. I was stunned. How could a country that an athlete was going to represent, the proudest country in the world, not want to provide everything necessary for that athlete to succeed? The kids needed me, why was this happening?

I begged and pleaded, and finally I was allowed to stay in the Pavilion. I was not, however, allowed anywhere near the floor. So I spent each day sneaking around the floor area, trying to help my gymnasts as best I could. Usually, Mary Lou, Julianne, and I met behind the stands for last-minute pep talks and coaching. At night,

I tried to find places to sleep. I had not received a pass into the Olympic Village, so I had to rely on friends and on my own ingenuity. I was lucky to find Carol.

Carol was the piano player for the compulsory portion of the competition (no player was used for the optionals). He was also a Rumanian and a good friend from the '76 Olympics. For several nights I stayed in Carol's hotel room. When it was time for him to leave, he pulled me aside. "Bela," he said, "you can no longer stay at my hotel, but I am not going to return the car that the Federation loaned me. Take the car, here are the keys, and when they call me I'll tell them to call you, and you tell them to call me . . . we'll just send them back and forth for as long as we can."

That was Carol, bless his heart. I miss him a lot. I took his little car, and that's where I lived until the competition was over. I will never forget. Several nights I parked on the streets, but I was always nervous because people could see me through the windows. One night I parked in a secure parking lot ($2 during the day). I thought, gosh, I'm safe tonight. I opened my window a bit and went to sleep.

That night I had a bad, bad dream. I was in the gymnasium and the parallel bars had fallen while Mary Lou was performing on them. I was trapped beneath the bars, straining to hold them up so that Mary Lou wouldn't fall. I was screaming, "Hold on, Mary Lou, hold on to the bar!" I was desperate to save her from falling. I looked up to see her and I couldn't because there were bright lights shining in my eyes. I was desperate, sweating, and I was trying to hold up a piece of the broken bar. . . . Then I heard a voice and opened my eyes. "What are you doing here?" I still couldn't see because the lights were blinding me. Then I saw the man, a policeman, in front of me holding a flashlight in my face. I lied about who I was and why I was there and the policeman let me go. I drove to another parking lot. It was just part of the nightmare, and part of the reality of the '84 Games.

But it was a beautiful competition. Mary Lou and Kati Szabo fought fiercely. Up and down, one in the lead and then the other. It was difficult to watch Kati and the others on her team and not feel a pang of sadness. They were a piece of my past, and I was emotionally tied to them. I knew when each one was nervous, how to loosen their muscles, and the words to say to give them the confidence to excel.

I have always been a strategist. In my mind, I am always thinking about how to take advantage of an opponent's weakness. I did not want to take advantage of Kati and the others—I knew them too well. How in the world, I wondered, was I going to handle my past relationship with the Rumanian team? I decided that I had to block them out. I could not feel for them because it would bring me back again. I had to be a professional and stand strong behind Mary Lou and Julianne. It was very hard.

Everything came down to the last event. Mary Lou had received a 9.85 on the bars. That wasn't the high score that she had expected. She hadn't made any major mistakes, but she had lost her balance for a moment on her Retton salto. The salto is a move where she flips from the lower to the upper bar and lands, seated, with her arms outstretched on the top bar. Going into her final event, the vault, Mary Lou was trailing Kati by five-hundredths of a point. A 9.95 would tie her with Kati for first in the all-around. Only a perfect 10 would allow Mary Lou to win.

I did not tell Mary Lou that she needed a 10. I told her only the words I felt she needed to hear to become a champion. "Here is the vault of your life," I said. "Be strong and aggressive, don't hold anything back. Do a vault like you have never done in your life— push it hard." "Yes, yes," Mary Lou responded, "I'm going to do that." "Mary Lou, this vault must be done very beautifully, and you can do a beautiful vault. Don't forget, go flat into the horse, straight and strong."

Mary Lou had some difficulty getting enough height from her vaults for a good landing. In order to land perfectly, she needed to hit the vault with enough force to generate height. As we looked into each other's faces, we both knew what she needed to do. "I'll show them," Mary Lou promised, and moved toward the floor.

To give a gymnast the mental power, confidence, and capability to put forward an ultimate effort at the time when everybody else is shaking is everything. Nadia developed that power and capability. So did Mary Lou.

When Mary Lou hit the vault, her ferocity and strength sent her sailing. She whirled through the air and then landed, *puck*, no step back. The applause sounded like thunder. I ran toward the forbidden barrier and leapt onto the floor. Mary Lou raced toward me and jumped into my arms. The scoreboard flashed 10, but she didn't know that meant she had won. "One more good one," she said to me with a grin and headed over for her next vault. I gave her a huge bear hug as her second 10 appeared on the board and the news that she was the 1984 all-around Olympic Champion boomed from the loudspeakers. "We did it, Bela," she said as we whirled in circles.

Don Peters rushed me like a wounded animal. He attempted to push me off the floor, but he was too late. The arena had erupted with applause and the competition was over. Mary Lou had become the first American gymnast ever to win a gold in the all-around competition. Her final score, 79.175 to Kati's 79.125, had ensured her place in history. I had been there to support and coach Mary Lou, despite Peters's efforts to keep me away. Julianne also became an Olympic Champion on the bars and a silver medalist on the floor.

I did not confront Peters after the Games. "Hey," I said to him in '84, "you do whatever you want. You are the power here, the one who got voted into power by your clan, and you have the authority. I am only here to help the kids." I tried not to pay attention to Peters, or to anyone else who didn't like me or what I was doing. That type of intrigue is draining, it takes away from the important things—like preparation.

Many times I have asked myself how I could have better handled the situation with Don Peters. I realize now that my presence in the Pavilion was very threatening to him. It must have been unpleasant to have a powerful coach, the one who put the best kids on the floor, in the arena. But that should not have been the issue.

In 1984 the Federation supported the wishes of a designated coach before the welfare of their own athletes. My own efforts for my kids and my new country were partly ignored. However, Mike Jacki did make a public statement to U.S. coaches about me following the Games. In answer to coaches who said I was getting too much attention Jacki stated that the reason no attention was being paid to some of the coaches was that they were too busy complaining about me, and focusing on sabotaging my efforts instead of on developing athletes. He told them that if they created world-class athletes they'd get the same attention. Bela's getting attention because his athletes are standing in the front row, Jacki said, not because everyone is sympathizing with him. He isn't the most popular person in the country, and he had no track record except in history, but he is producing athletes in the United States who create results. Create similar results and you will get the same attention.

The creation of Mary Lou Retton wasn't just the creation of an Olympic Champion. In her own way she made a contribution to the sport of gymnastics, just as Nadia had before her. Mary Lou opened the eyes of millions of young American kids to the beauty of her sport, and gave the final proof that U.S. gymnasts could be as good as anyone else.

Gymnastics became a craze in the United States. Before 1984 we had eight hundred students enrolled in our gym. Following the Games our numbers doubled. Thousands of kids joined clubs around the country. It was so ironic. For three years American coaches had been blaming me for everything wrong with the sport. Now, because of a gymnast I had developed into an Olympic Champion, they were getting more business than they had ever imagined. Nobody thanked me.

The 1984 Games awakened American gymnastics and gave Americans pride in their gymnasts and their country. The success of Mary Lou and Julianne pumped energy and money into the sport on a giant scale. There was a lot of positive activity. In the end, however, the 1984 Games forced me to face a painful reality: The same egos and bureaucracy, not the glory of the sport, persisted in both my native country and my new home. I swallowed a bitter pill that I have known all my life and did what I have always done— I turned to coach the new generation of gymnasts, still harboring the dream that next time it might be different.

22.

Why Me?

I became a coach because I wanted to give something to the kids who had nothing. I wanted to be a positive influence, a leader, and to both give and receive respect based on what was deserved. I had never received encouragement as a young athlete. Sometimes I desperately needed a kind word, a pat on the head, or someone to share my concerns with. I was determined to give those things to my kids.

A coach is not a puppet or a robot fulfilling a paid obligation. He or she has to be much more than that. Coaching is a profession. A coach doesn't just spot stunts. He is an educator, a motivator, a disciplinarian, and a loyal supporter. I confess that I believe you must have a certain innate quality to be a coach. It's like an artist having a natural talent.

Coaches are role models for their athletes. I am a strong believer in the idea that how a coach acts in his private life, off the floor, is how he should expect his athletes to act. If I am a person who is late, who comes to workouts unprepared, my eyes big like onions, drunk as a skunk, or spaced out from a late night or fatigue, I can't expect my athletes to act differently. The kids watch closely. They take in your mental state and moral standards and respond accordingly. If they consider you a person of integrity, then they will follow you through fire.

As a coach it is part of the job not to be shy of the public. If a coach is afraid of the public, he is in the wrong profession. Coaching is like being an actor: You have to perform in front of an audience. You have to perform without caring about how you look, thinking only of your athlete. A coach has to work to make the spectators aware of any judging errors in order to have them corrected. The only important thing is being aware of what is happening in a competition, what is happening to your athletes.

I have a well-known style in competitions. When there is an injustice that hurts my athletes I yell, I pound the table. I fight for my gymnasts' rights. I fight to get the audience to recognize those rights and to raise their voices with my own. Sometimes it works, sometimes it doesn't, but I would never let an injustice go without a fight. I have never been bashful in front of the audience; I have never tried to hide my emotions. I am comfortable in a fight, I feel I have a chance to win.

When I came to the United States it was painful to learn that, here, anybody can be a coach. No specific college education is needed. Anyone can decide, hey, tomorrow I am going to be a coach because my child is involved in gymnastics, or I have nothing better to do. All a prospective coach needs is enough money to open a little shack or a studio. Without education, knowledge, or an understanding of the proper mental and physical standards needed to become a coach, a person can hang out a shingle.

Hundreds of opportunity-seeking organizations around the country operate with little know-how. During my travels I have met a lot of people who offer services they don't understand. They have found a hiding place within the sport, and their efforts damage us all. Those individuals lower the reputation of the coaching community, the prestige of being a coach, and the public's appreciation of the sport.

I came from a country where you could not be a physical education teacher or coach without a university diploma. That diploma involved four years at a university to be a physical education teacher, and two additional years of specialized training in a chosen field before you could be named a coach. Six years of training, and without that training, and the resulting diploma, no one would even think of hiring you to teach or coach.

In Rumania, a coaching career was highly respected. Sports were among the most efficient moral and physical education tools for the young generation. Sports created discipline, entertainment, and idols. Shortly after I came to the United States, I learned the pros and cons of sports in my former country compared to sports in the United States. While I miss the prestige involved in coaching in Rumania, I value the freedom I have gained in the United States to organize my gymnastics club without government intervention. The opportunity to create a gymnastics program based on healthy principles, and to work with athletes who are focused on achieving the same goals as my own, makes up for the decrease in recognition and appreciation that coaches receive in the United States.

In the end, it is about my relationships with my gymnasts. It's about working together, working toward mutual personal and professional fulfillment. When Mary Lou flew toward me after her second perfect vault in the 1984 Olympics she yelled, "Bela, we've done it; we've done it!" Not "I've done it." Mary Lou recognized, instinctively, that our common efforts had generated her ultimate success. Our efforts had created the first U.S. all-around Olympic Champion.

I have always felt very strongly that the only thing my gymnasts owe me is respect based on reciprocity. I will never forget when Mary Lou won the '84 all-around Olympic title, and I had the opportunity to help her make the transition from a person to a sports personality. "Mary Lou," I said, "from now on everyone will want a piece of you. They will want to touch you, speak with you, market you, and you have to decide the person you will be. You must keep your feet on the ground if you want to survive."

It was relatively easy to help Mary Lou keep control of her life, because she continued to practice and compete with our club after the Games. She maintained her disciplined life, and that helped her to cope with the new demands placed on her. I knew that she would need help managing her career, so I contacted a sports agent and arranged a meeting.

When I met with the sports agent, he told me that he would divide up whatever income Mary Lou made with his agency in the following way: 75 percent would go to Mary Lou, 25 percent would go to him. Then he said to me, "Bela, what percentage of Mary Lou's income do you want?" I had not thought about it, but I answered 10 percent from his 25 percent if Mary Lou and her parents agreed to the contract.

I arranged a meeting with the Rettons, the agent, and myself. The Rettons agreed to have the agent represent Mary Lou's interest. When all the papers were signed, I turned to Mary Lou. "Mary Lou," I said, "I have one final gift to give you." I took my pen and signed my 10 percent over to her. That meant that Mary Lou would receive 85 percent of any money she made through her work with that agent. That was one of the most favorable sports contracts any athlete had ever received.

I didn't want 10 percent of Mary Lou's income. She had given me years of joy, deep professional satisfaction, and a sense of pride as the result of her Olympic success. That was all she owed me. I did not want money to come between us. I wanted to keep her friendship for the rest of my life. I wanted to be a part of her future with no strings attached. And I am.

That is what being a coach is about.

23.

The Five

After the 1984 Olympics I returned to the gym to coach our next generation of champions. There were five—Kristie Phillips, Phoebe Mills, Chelle Stack, Rhonda Faehn, and Brandy Johnson. Instead of a cohesive group, we had five young girls with such different personalities and family backgrounds that the goal of channeling them into a team was extremely difficult.

Kristie Phillips was a born showgirl. She had the ability to play with the crowd, as well as with individuals. She was a very coordinated gymnast with great flexibility and excellent competitive capabilities. And her mother would do anything possible to help Kristie achieve success. They were not wealthy people, and I always admired the love that motivated Mrs. Phillips to make any sacrifice for Kristie's career. It was unfortunate that Kristie did not always seem to grasp or thoroughly appreciate her mother's feelings or sacrifices.

We used to call Phoebe Mills "Phobiscus." She was like a tiny mosquito—so small and delicate. Phoebe never showed great joy or great pain. She was a sturdy engine, going, going, going. She was the ultimate worker, a disciplined person, but she was not the ultimate competitor. The fierceness of competition, the public's reactions, all affected her performances. She was, however, one of the hardest-working gymnasts I ever knew, and I appreciated and admired her efforts.

Then there was Chelle Stack. I first spoke with Chelle's parents when they called me after the '84 Olympics and asked me to fly to the Midwest to see their nine-year-old daughter perform. They told me that Chelle was incredibly talented, and was training with a famous Russian coach. They said I simply had to come to see their child. I said, "Excuse me, but that is not the way we do things. If you would like to bring Chelle to our facility in Houston, I would be more than happy to look at her." I didn't hear from the Stacks for quite some time.

One day we had a competition in the Midwest, and the Stacks showed up. They asked me to come to their gym and watch Chelle perform. I had some time after the competition so I went. Chelle was a little bitty girl—very light looking—a toy in the hands of her coach. The Russian fellow turned her, hand over hand, in all her tumbling efforts. I told the Stacks that I needed to see how Chelle could do without a spotter. They informed me that she was hurt, but on a normal basis she could do all her tumbling without a spot. They asked me what I thought. "Well," I began, "I cannot make a judgment without seeing your child perform up to her capabilities— based on her own efforts." I did not hear from the Stacks for a while.

I immediately recognized them when they arrived at my gym. Chelle was in tow. "We've brought our daughter to train with Mary Lou," the Stacks informed me. "Well," I said, "she won't train with Mary Lou, but we can start her at the next lower level." That began what I can only call a difficult relationship.

Chelle was a tiny child, very dynamic but emotionally fragile and inconsistent. Her behavior in practice was emotional and petulant. In competition, she would come up with strange mistakes that she'd never made before. She would mess up and fail without apparent reason.

Frank and Carol Stack would take Chelle from the gym and disappear a month at a time—once we did not see them for several months. Then they would return as if nothing had happened. Our policy is to never close our doors to anyone, so we always took Chelle back. I felt sorry for the child, and despite her difficult personality, I could not bring myself to eliminate her from our program. However, at one point I told the Stacks, "Chelle will not make the Olympic team if you keep fooling around," I began. "You are confusing the child, and you are confusing yourselves. You are chasing phantoms that you will never reach. Chelle needs consistent preparation—let her alone. Just let her alone to prepare. Stop hovering around each practice and pulling her from the gym whenever you feel like it . . . just let her be." For a time things went well.

Rhonda Faehn was never, never a problem. Rhonda was thirteen years old when she came to the gym. Her family could barely afford to bring her to Houston, yet they put Rhonda's interests before their own—they were caring, loving people. Beginning at a young age, Rhonda had taken care of herself. I have never worked with a more disciplined and controlled child. She was serious, hard working, and the ultimate competitor. She was not a super talent, but she never made mistakes. She never failed to complete her routines, and she always provided a plus to every competition. What's more, Rhonda never complained. She would have put her hand through fire for her teammates. That was why Rhonda was always our opener—the backbone of our team.

As I've mentioned, the opener in team competitions is the sacrificial lamb. It takes a certain personality to fill that position. That gymnast must be mentally strong, smart, and physically accomplished. She must also be willing to let the glory go to someone else on the team without feeling left out or used. Rhonda was a true team player. Her contributions over the years made the difference between gold and silver. She was a joy to work with and I will always admire her.

Brandy Johnson came to us in 1987. She and her mother moved to Houston from Florida. A powerful young person, she was very similar in quality to Mary Lou—fast, quick, and strong. But, despite her natural talent Brandy was a breaker during competitions. It was frustrating for me to see her ability, and watch it go to waste when she broke.

Mental strength comes with constant training and direction. I knew, with Brandy, it would be a desparate race with time to get her consistent and confident enough to excel in the Olympic Games. She did, however, rapidly improve and began to compete strongly. When it came time for the Olympic Trials, Brandy had established herself as one of the leading personalities on the national team. She came a long way in a short time, and we were all very proud of her.

Kristie, Phoebe, Chelle, Rhonda, and Brandy. The road to the 1988 Olympics was full of victories, defeats, frustrations, and elations. In the beginning, the kids were young, and we began by competing in 1985 at the Junior National level. That first year Kristie won the Junior elite division and Phoebe placed second. Then it was time for the American Cup, my very favorite competition.

The American Cup always brings back memories of Nadia's first international success in 1976 at the first edition of the Cup. It was in New York's Madison Square Garden that Nadia, a tiny, unknown little girl, gave a memorable performance and became the first winner of the Cup. Only a few months later, Nadia became the all-around Olympic Champion at the 1976 games in Montreal. Through the years, the American Cup has become a stepping-stone for gymnasts, providing increased visibility and propelling them to Olympic greatness. Nadia's story was repeated in 1983, when Mary Lou Retton won the Cup in a spectacular victory that put her in the spotlight for the upcoming 1984 Olympics. And then, in 1986, it was time for Kristie Phillips to repeat history. I had to fight just as fiercely as in Nadia's and Mary Lou's cases to introduce Kristie in the Cup. There was opposition from the Federation and its national team coach, Don Peters. But I managed to introduce Kristie, and she turned my efforts into her own golden opportunity.

Before the final portion of the 1986 American Cup, Kristie Phillips turned to me and said, "I can win this." I was shocked. So much confidence in a thirteen-year-old little girl who had only won one junior-level championship. But by the end of the competition that little kid was a household name. It was her back-breaking flexibility (a reverse planche) on the beam that caught the media's fancy and the gymnastic community's attention. That, and the fact that Kristie never just executed a routine, she performed it. Kristie was an artist, and she would strut and sell her stuff. She played the crowd like a pro. After she won the American Cup, Kristie was unstoppable. She went on to win the Senior Nationals, and four gold medals, including the all-around title, at the U.S. Olympic Festival in Houston.

Things were going too well. Then, a few months before the Senior National Championship in 1988, Kristie disappeared. No explanation, no goodbye. It was the Diane Durham story all over again. Kristie left, without a word, and she and her mother moved to California—to be coached by Don Peters. Peters was still the national team coach. That meant he would be the coach for the 1988 Olympics. I believe that Kristie and her mother felt that if they went to Peters's facility for coaching, Kristie would be a shoo-in for the Olympic team. The Phillips's move was not a smart one.

Kristie Phillips was already the American Cup Champion. She had proved her merit in the Nationals and countless other competitions. She did not need any political help to make the Olympic team. We were surprised when Kristie left, but we understood. Once again vulnerability and speculation of both the parent and child had caused them to make a major mistake. The Senior Nationals were on hand, and we focused on the preparation of our remaining gymnasts.

Kristie Phillips's performance in the 1988 Senior Nationals was disastrous. She placed ninth in the competition. Phoebe won the all-around, and Chelle and Brandy placed fourth and sixth, respectively. It hadn't taken long for Kristie to lose her conditioning, her self-control, or her discipline. Working with a gymnast is not just a question of orders or format, it's not the placement of objects, it's the mind-set, the mental influence—the words, the tone, the short comments or long discussions. It's about finding what works. No two coaches work in the same fashion, just as no two carpenters do. But two coaches can work with the same gymnasts and one will create a failure and one a success.

When Kristie Phillips returned to our gym she was in a difficult situation. As always, our doors remained open and we took her back. Kristie was overweight and we worked hard to get her weight down and to regain her physical fitness. Slowly her routines improved and a few days before the Trials she was back in shape.

Kristie Phillips nearly broke herself in two in her efforts to regain her strength and endurance. But it didn't matter, because the rumors of Kristie's downfall had already traveled around the country. As had happened in the past, people with certain priorities representing coaching or judging organizations acted unfairly. In a particularly blatant conflict of interest, Audrey Schweyer—who was affiliated with the Parkettes Club in Allentown, Pennsylvania—was named a judge of the competition.

Going into the Olympic Trials we had five gymnasts who would most likely make the team. Of the five, Rhonda and Kristie were the weakest at the time. Rhonda, however, was a world-class vaulter by that point, and still the best opener that the Olympic team could hope for. Kristie had made an amazing comeback. While these two were at that moment the weakest on our team, they were still high above the rest of their direct competition for a place on the team.

Five gymnasts from my club. It was too much for Peters, Schweyer, and the rest of the opposition to handle. Peters, still the national team coach, didn't even have one gymnast who could touch my kids. The Trials were a nightmare. Kristie's and Rhonda's scores were cut so low it was unbelievable. I cried at the injustice. *"How in the world, how in the world,"* I shouted, *"can this happen in a civilized country?"*

In the end, Phoebe Mills won the all-around; Brandy placed fourth; Chelle, fifth; and Kristie Phillips, the former National Champion of the United States, ended up in eighth place, one place short of being named an alternate for the Olympic team. Rhonda Faehn placed seventh—and was named first alternate.

We were all supposed to be working toward the same goal: the strongest gymnastics team for the '88 Olympic Games. The elimination of Kristie was not only cruel but a waste. Even if Kristie had only been strong on the beam she belonged on the Olympic team. Her beam routine was spectacular and complex, one of the best in the world, and she was virtually guaranteed to bring home a medal in that event. In addition, she was an excellent floor performer, a decent vaulter, and a good bar performer. She would have helped the team, as well as the overall medal count for the U.S.

Two athletes at the 1988 Trials were taught valuable lessons. Kristie and Rhonda learned that hard work, stupendous talent, and rigorous discipline meant nothing to the shallow individuals sitting on the panel of judges.

Immediately following the competition a rule, set in stone, came down from the Federation. The first alternate could not be used during the competition unless a gymnast stepped out or was injured. That meant that even though Rhonda was far more important and valuable to the team than another who was competing, the Olympic team coach could not substitute her. The reason for that rule was clear: Had Rhonda been allowed to compete, I would have had four gymnasts from my club on the team—a majority. That would have challenged both Don Peters's authority and the validity of his position as coach of the Olympic team.

I challenged the validity of Don Peters's position as the Olympic team coach anyway. I did not challenge him because I wanted to be the Olympic coach. I challenged him because my kids needed my coaching in Seoul, Korea, and I wanted the right to coach them on the floor, not from behind the bleachers. I refused to stay in my car again!

The Federation tried to appease me, and to avoid a scandal. They offered Marta the position of "assistant Olympic coach" and they offered me a position as "head of the gymnastics delegation." Head of the delegation? *Pah*, that wouldn't allow me on the floor to coach my kids. Peters didn't have one of his gymnasts on the team, why should he be allowed on the floor and not me?

The media picked up the controversy. "Hey, wait a second," the media began to write, "why should Peters go to Seoul when he doesn't even have one of his own gymnasts on the team?" They began to recall the '84 Olympics. They remembered Peters pushing me off the floor during those memorable moments of Mary Lou's victory. They began to write about the way Peters tried to take credit for the work of other coaches.

Peters defended his position. He claimed that he had been elected, true enough—but by a handful of his own friends. But that wasn't really the point. The point was that the kids needed their own coaches. I wasn't fighting to get Peters to resign, I was fighting for the rights of all the kids to have their individual coaches present and coaching them both prior to and during the Olympics.

In a month's time, I wouldn't have been able to figure out what made any other gymnast tick. It takes years to understand a gymnast.

To know how to praise or chastise her efforts, to know what works, and to instill confidence and inspire her toward monumental efforts. I knew how to touch my gymnasts, to boost their ambitions. I knew how to turn on those red engines. Every gymnast is different—some hate to be shaken up, some need a strong hand. It's the things that are never written on their faces that are the most important. That's why it is vital that gymnasts have their own coaches next to them during the most important moments of their athletic careers.

I believe that the ensuing controversy became embarrassing for Peters. His position began to look foolish. Don eventually resigned as team coach. Following his resignation, the Federation began discussing who they were going to elect as the new Olympic coach. They called me for the job. "What are you talking about?" I said. "We just got out of one type of system and you want to reinvent our problems? You want to elect me for the next four or five years? Who knows what kind of contribution I'll make toward the team in one year let alone five. My interest is solely in providing coaching services for my own athletes."

I consider what happened next as my greatest political success on the organization side of gymnastics. At my insistence, a rule was introduced in 1988 that allowed gymnasts to have their own coaches on the floor during the Olympics. Every individual athlete from that point on could have their own coach.

I commend the Federation for finally having the guts to break with tradition in the interest of the kids. And I suppose it is to their credit that the U.S. Gymnastics Federation felt frustrated about the elimination of Kristie Phillips. In the end, they promised her that she would be sent to Seoul, at the Federation's expense, with the rest of the team despite her eighth-place finish. Unfortunately, that was a promise they couldn't keep. The Federation did not have the authority to make that promise. The United States Olympic Committee had the last word on who went and who didn't. They gave out the credentials to each individual participating in an event.

Kristie was not participating, so she could not get the credentials necessary to make the trip.

Up until the last moment Kristie thought she was going to Seoul. It wasn't much compensation for having her place on the team stolen from her, but it kept her spirits from plummeting. On the day before we left for Seoul a messenger from the Federation told Kristie that she couldn't make the trip. Kristie and her mother did not take the news well.

There was nothing I could do. I packed my bags and left for Seoul.

24.

Nightmare 1988

The 1988 Olympics in Seoul, South Korea, were a nightmare—a downward spiral that began with the elimination of Kristie Phillips and the placement of Rhonda Faehn as an alternate who could never be used—and those were the high points. Everyone knows that we were sent home without the bronze medal that we felt my kids had won. That medal was ripped from the necks of the U.S. gymnasts by Ellen Berger, the former East German head of the women's technical committee for the International Gymnastics Federation.

Going into 1988 we faced the general aggression of the Germans. It was clear that the Rumanians and the Soviets would battle for the gold and the silver. The Germans knew that we stood between them and the bronze medal. A medal they had historically won. They knew that they would have to beat us. Throughout the podium workouts we maintained our superiority. We gave the general impression that we were in control and that the situation was favorable

Bela's godmother, Maria, and Bela. *Bela Karolyi Archives.*

Bela and sister, Maria. *Bela Karolyi Archives.*

Bela instructing Nadia. *Ion Mihaica.*

Bela spotting Nadia during the 1973 London Championship. *Bela Karolyi Archives.*

Bela and daughter Andrea.
Bela Karolyi Archives.

Nadia. *Bela Karolyi Archives.*

ABOVE: The first gymnastics show in Vulcan and Lupeni. *Bela Karolyi Archives*. RIGHT: Nadia, winner of the 1972 Friendship Cup. *Karl-Heinz Friedrich*. BELOW: Nadia's generation in Onesti in 1968. *Bela Karolyi Archives*.

TOP: Teadora Ungureanu and Nadia Comaneci with Bela after the 1976 Olympics. *Bela Karolyi Archives.* ABOVE LEFT: Kim and Bela – last instructions before going to the beam. *Dave Black.* ABOVE RIGHT: Bela and Kim Zmeskal enjoying the victory after the 1991 World Championships. *Dave Black.*

TOP LEFT: Betty Okino performing at the 1991 World Championships in Indianapolis. *Dave Black*. TOP RIGHT: Mary Lou Retton on the balance beam leaping toward the 1984 Olympic All-Around Title. *Dave Black*. ABOVE: Kristie Phillips performing her famous move – "the Phillips." *Dave Black*.

BELOW: Kim Zmeskal, graceful as always on the beam. *Dave Black.*
BOTTOM LEFT: Phoebe Mills – Olympic bronze medalist on the beam. *Dave Black.*
BOTTOM RIGHT: Hilary Grivich – the sturdy-as-iron beamer. *Dave Black.*

RIGHT: Bela with his champions – a grown-up Nadia, Mary Lou Retton, and Kim Zmeskal. *Debbie VanHorn.*
BELOW: Bela celebrates Kim Zmeskal's victory at the 1991 World Championships. *Dave Black.*
INSET: Bela gives Kim Zmeskal some last minute instruction at the 1991 World Championships. *Dave Black.*

ABOVE LEFT: Betty Okino gets positive reinforcement from Bela before she begins her floor routine. *Dave Black.*

ABOVE RIGHT: Bela gives Kim Zmeskal advice before a beam routine. *Dave Black.*

BELOW: A team competition meeting – Bela makes sure his gymnasts are ready to fight like tigers. *Dave Black.*

for us. This impression was recognized by the officials of all the participating countries.

The team was strong, but we had some problems. We had no outstanding opener. Rhonda stood with the team, but we could not use her. We also had no clincher, no famous star. Kristie was gone, and we had to use Phoebe Mills as our sixth performer in each event. Phoebe was well prepared and disciplined, but she was not a Nadia or a Mary Lou. Brandy was improving and looked strong, but she had no international name yet. Chelle was a wild-card. I did not know the other gymnasts on our team well enough to begin to predict where they would succeed or break. Those gymnasts included Missy Marlowe, from Rocky Mountain Gym; Hope Spivey, from Parkettes Club; and the talented Kelly Garrison, from the University of Oklahoma.

The compulsories went well—that is, they went well except for one hitch. Chelle Stack fell off the bars during her compulsory. She went into a handstand and then she lost control, she pulled back, pushed over, and fell from her handstand. Dammit. Her score was eliminated.

At the end of the compulsories we were solidly in third place. And we were ecstatic. We were ahead of the Germans and within a few tenths of the Rumanians—we never expected to be that close to a silver medal. Friends rushed down from the stands to congratulate the kids and to wish us well in the optionals. It was a victory for us.

As we walked toward the locker rooms we heard a lot of yells and cheers from the stands and we stopped for a moment to wave to our supporters. Then we moved toward the tunnel that led to the locker room. There, directly above the tunnel was a person just waving like crazy. I looked at the person's face and saw that it was Chelle Stack's father. I smiled and waved—I assumed he was also congratulating us.

"*Hey! Hey, you stole my child's medal,*" Frank Stack screamed at me. *"You made her go third during the compulsories, and that's why she fell off the bars. If you'd put her sixth she would have felt more comfortable and she wouldn't have fallen."* I stared at him. The idea that if she'd been placed sixth she wouldn't have fallen was a cruel joke.

"You stole, you stole my child's medal . . ." "You jerk," I screamed in my mind to Frank. "You have no idea what you're saying. You have no idea what damage you are doing to your own daughter. I cannot do anything about that, but you are also hurting all the people around you." We walked through the tunnel. It was like a cold shower. One moment we had all been celebrating, the next we were quiet. That was one of the darkest moments as a coach that I remember. Chelle apologized the next morning for her father's outburst.

The day before the optionals word leaked out that Ellen Berger had held a judges' meeting during which she cautioned the judges not to allow the scores to elevate as the night of the optionals progressed. This would have been a fairly normal occurrence, except that East Germany, Ellen Berger's country, was performing in the first rotation of the day. I knew then that the fight for the bronze would be a fight against Ellen Berger. I had clashed with Ellen many times in the past, and anyone could see that it would be difficult for her to let anyone else walk out with the bronze medal.

We began the optional portion of the competition. We maintained our third-place position until the bars. I asked Rhonda to pull the springboard away from the bars after Kelly Garrison began her routine. Rhonda pulled the board away and crouched silently on the floor behind it so the judges' view was not blocked. Kelly finished her routine and the rotation ended. That's when Berger raced down from her chair to the judging panel for the bars and made a ruling that lacked any kind of decency.

Berger, citing an unheard-of regulation which said that it is illegal for another person to remain on the podium during a performance, deducted a half point from the U.S. team's score. Five-tenths of a point is a mountain in gymnastics. I appealed to Yuri Titov, the president of the International Gymnastics Federation. I told him the only person on the podium was Rhonda, another gymnast, and that did not break any rule. Yuri just backed Berger and told me that since he hadn't seen the case he couldn't do anything about the deduction. The injustice was unbelievable! What could we do, Berger was the final word.

I wasn't surprised by Berger's ruling. I had known that if the German team's medal was threatened, she would try something. I was prepared for adversity. What was unacceptable, and what I was unprepared for, was the way the American delegation "defended" our rights.

Nobody stepped in. Highway robbery, and nothing was done. The U.S. Olympic Delegation leader, the one who could have intervened and placed an official protest, did nothing but make promises that saw no results. No one said, wait a second, this is an international crime, an injustice, and I've got to stop it. I had a sense of déjà vu. We were being mistreated, robbed, and I was the only one defending the rights of the kids. I couldn't find one person from the U.S. delegation to stand up and defend the rights of our athletes.

Paul Ziert came over to me after Berger's ruling and said, "Bela, it's the same old thing. It's just like you went through in 1980. You can't do anything about it, huh?" "No, Paul," I answered. "I am once again with my hands tied and my words falling on deaf ears." We tried to talk with the media, to get them to publicly challenge Berger, but nothing worked. Without a statement from the delegation denouncing Berger's ruling, without a protest or a threat to withdraw our team, nobody would listen. A crying shame.

We did not accept defeat. We continued to fight, each gymnast performing to the best of her capabilities and executing superior routines. Still, despite the initial official results on the arena scoreboard, which showed that the American team was the bronze medal winner, the East German team was awarded that medal. Ellen Berger's penalty had taken the U.S. gymnasts' medal away.

The kids were devastated. How could I explain to them that what had happened wasn't their fault? "You guys," I said, "you have to be proud. Whatever was done was according to your best capabilities. The medal was taken off your necks, but you still won that medal. I know that, you know that, and everyone in the world gymnastics community knows that." Our fourth-place finish was still the best all-around finish that had ever been achieved by a U.S. Olympic team in an Olympic Games with full participation of the world gymnastic community. "You have your memories, and have accomplished one of the greatest achievements in U.S. sports history," I told the kids.

I believed in what I said to the team, but my words were also touched by the sadness and frustration that we all felt. Ellen Berger's actions were brutal. What she did should not have happened in a civilized Olympic Games.

In a sense, I always accepted Ellen and the way she fought for her country. I, too, fight without reservation for my team. I fought for Rumania, and I now fight for the United States. But with Ellen it is different. Her fighting is detrimental to everyone else. It locks everyone else's chances out, and I condemn that type of action.

I do not believe Berger felt any remorse for her actions that day. She took pride in both her achievement and her country's medal. So much pride that she personally presented her team the bronze during the awards ceremony. My kids cried as Ellen Berger moved toward the podium to place bronze medals on the necks of the East German gymnasts.

Rhonda Faehn was probably scarred the most by Ellen Berger. Rhonda was a sensitive person. She never showed her emotions in practice or competitions, but this time she was hurt beyond the limit. Up until that point no one would have been as dedicated to her team or as disciplined with herself as Rhonda. Even though everyone around, except Marta and me, had told her she would not have a chance to compete in the Olympics, she performed until the last moment in Seoul at all of the podium workouts. Not only did she practice, she improved.

When the competition began and it was clear that Rhonda would not compete, she quietly, without any sort of tantrum, supported her teammates all the way to the end. There were no reproaches, no jealous words. Through the years it is easy to exaggerate a memory, but I am not mistaken in my thoughts of Rhonda. I have never seen a gymnast with such moral integrity. Her attitude was generated by a sturdy, organized life and self-discipline, and proba- bly the knowledge that nobody could help her but herself. Ellen Berger's ruling could not have been aimed at a more undeserving target.

There was, however, also a high point in the Games. A beautiful fight for the bronze on the beam by Phoebe Mills. Phoebe was in fifth place. There was a very slight chance that anyone could move in front of the athletes already in first through fourth place. Yet one by one they made small mistakes and a narrow gap was opened for Phoebe.

Even though Phoebe wasn't a pressure performer, on that day she executed flawless move after move on the beam. It was like God wanted to reward her for all her hard work. When her score flashed across the board she had moved from fifth to third. Phoebe Mills had won the individual bronze on the beam. It was so nice to happen—for her, for the rest of the team, and for Marta and me. We were very proud of Phoebe, and she was moved and satisfied.

I was also very proud of Brandy Johnson's performance. She hit all her routines without any hesitation or mistake. She didn't win a medal, but she showed spectacular improvement. She gave a strong, very confident performance in Seoul. Brandy went to Seoul as an unknown and was scored accordingly.

We returned to Houston. Rhonda was still working out but had begun to focus on college. She had been offered, and had accepted, a full scholarship to UCLA. Kristie had quit gymnastics. Brandy was still practicing after a brief time away from the gym, and Phoebe continued to train although she was a bit tired from the strain of the Olympics. Chelle and her family disappeared.

The U.S. Gymnastics Federation called me to organize the girls for a big post-Olympic tournament to travel around the country. So we began to get the kids back in shape. A few days before the tour I was at my ranch hanging some antique snowshoes on the wall when I fell off my ladder. I broke my hand very badly and went to the hospital for surgery as the kids began their tour.

By the time the tour ended, Brandy had left our gym to return to Florida to train. I was disappointed. I am normally a fighter, but I felt depressed. I missed Rhonda's presence, and I was saddened by Kristie's departure from the sport. But most of all I was hurt by Brandy's move. I had viewed Brandy as the next big Olympic champion, the one who was really coming up on the international stage. She did not continue with gymnastics for very long after she left our club.

Then there was Phoebe. She had been diagnosed with mononucleosis, and it had gotten worse and worse. Poor thing, she was really dragging. I met with Mr. and Mrs. Mills, and we discussed Phoebe's situation. Her parents are very nice people. Phoebe's father is a lawyer and an intelligent and athletic man. He has a clear understanding about what the athletic life is all about. We all decided that Phoebe needed a break. She needed time to rest and to visit with her family.

Phoebe went home. One day she called and said, "Bela, what would you think if I tried a new sport?" "What do you have in mind?" I asked. "Well, I think I'd like to try diving," she answered. I told her that I thought diving would be very nice, a new experience. "You would be so fortunate," I said, "to have two different sports in your life which you love and in which you can excel. I would advise you, if you have the chance and you feel the desire, go for it, experience something new." I was sorry to lose Phoebe, but proud that she turned to me for advice—that showed her respect for me, the sport, and our relationship as coach and athlete.

I knew when Phoebe left that it was time once again to focus on the next generation. They were to be one of the most positive, adorable groups of young kids I have ever worked with. I called them the Pumpkin Generation.

25.

Big Mama

H ere comes big Mama with a little bitty kid hanging onto her hand. "Where's Mary Lou?" Mama asks. "There she is, there she is," she says and pulls her daughter forward to watch. "What is your name?" she asks me. "My name is Bela," I answer, knowing what will come next. "This is my daughter, can you tell me how long it will take for her to become a champion?" I tell her that it takes quite a while. "Well, I want you to know that my daughter can do everything Mary Lou Retton does—even more. When does the Olympic thing happen?" I tell her that it is a few years away. "That's too long," she tells me, "can we move it up?"

I try to bring them back to reality. I tell those mothers that we have a long way to go. They don't want to listen, but I keep talking. "Listen up," I begin in a soft, conspiratorial whisper, "it doesn't matter what's going to happen. No, no, no, just listen for a moment. Your daughter is already a winner, she's already a champion. At the time you brought her in, at the time you agreed to support her athletic interest in gymnastics, she became a winner. You are about to give her something that money cannot buy."

Every sport has a certain amount of challenge. Some sports, like football and hockey, involve teammates. The responsibility for success or failure is shared. Then there are sports like cycling, skiing, or the bobsled. Once again success or failure is not solely the responsibility of the athlete. There is always something else that can be blamed. "It wasn't me that lacked preparation, it wasn't my mistake, my ski wasn't waxed correctly, my tire blew out, the snow wasn't fast enough." Then there is gymnastics.

In gymnastics there is nothing but the athlete. If her body does not respond correctly then that is her fault. There is ultimate satisfaction because the one responsible for the victory is the gymnast— no one else. That is why gymnastics develops such a sense of fulfillment. It also develops a unique self-discipline and self-confidence.

Gymnasts learn respect for their sport and for their fellow competitors. From the time they are four years old they know, and appreciate, the risk involved in performing stunts. They learn to work with their teammates and competitors in an extremely disciplined manner.

Gymnasts learn how to overcome difficulties, how to manage their time, and how to gain confidence. I tell Mama that her daughter will become a person who will set goals in her life and will know how to achieve them. That is the greatest prize that a parent could ever dream of—the gift of self-motivation.

The mamas don't always understand what I mean. Sometimes it takes years before they come back. When they do, they say, "Bela, back in the old days you told us to be proud of our kid. You said that she was going to be a winner, maybe not an immediate winner in gymnastics, but a winner in life. I thank God that we let her have that experience. She's growing like a weed, and we couldn't influence her life or her choices right now even if we tried to. But we don't have to try to influence her because she is a fighter with unbelievably high standards for herself. She's healthy and has direction. Her life is already a great success."

When I hear that I feel it in my heart. Because I know more than anyone else that I gave that child, and the children in the coal mining town of Vulcan, and the ones before and after, the light. I gave them the chance to be somebody. And when the media or anyone else attacks sports in general, especially gymnastics, I feel their words are criminal. It is a criminal attempt to cut off something that gives kids abilities money cannot buy.

There is, undeniably, pressure and stress in the world of competitive gymnastics. And it is true that American gymnasts are children, approximately thirteen to sixteen years old by the time they reach the elite levels. But they aren't your average teenagers. They are driven by their dreams—the hunger to win. No one twists their arms.

With few exceptions, American gymnasts are in the sport for themselves. The knocks they take, the pressure, the stress, can all be alleviated. At any time they are free to quit. Parents of teenagers know that it is hard enough to get their kids to clean their rooms, let alone practice in a gym four to eight hours a day. I am not a magician, I cannot make a child practice or perform if she doesn't have the desire and discipline. I wouldn't even want to try.

Don't feel sorry for elite gymnasts, assuming they have lost their childhood. That is a great mistake. Those gymnasts are the receivers, the ones who have cashed in on the efforts of hundreds of thousands of kids who have dreamed of sacrificing to become champions. Most celebrated gymnasts are gifted people who have come to that point through dedication and self-discipline. They are exceptional personalities and are lucky to have had the means and circumstances with which to reach their elevated status. They are not to be felt sorry for; they are to be applauded as role models and viewed as some of the strongest and luckiest individuals in the world.

26.

Reality

The reality is that after the Olympics you lose a generation. But that doesn't mean that a coach should retire with his students. After 1988, I returned to our gymnasium and began to work with a new group, among them Amanda Uherek, Erica Stokes, Amy Scheer, Hilary Grivich, Kerri Strug, and Kim Zmeskal. I called them the Pumpkin Generation. Such cute little kids, bless their hearts, an adorable bunch of nine- and ten-year-olds. Kim Zmeskal was the president of the Pumpkin Generation.

The new generation had only one problem: Chelle Stack had returned to our club. Chelle had gone to Don Peters's club in California following the Olympics, and things didn't work out well. She and her parents came to us to ask if they could return to our gym. I couldn't believe the Stacks had the nerve, after the way they had behaved in Seoul, to ask us to take Chelle back.

Marta did not want to let Chelle back into our club. It was the first time that we questioned our open-door policy. "Gosh," I said to Marta, "we have to give her a chance to be part of the club if she wants to." Marta responded, "Bela, you should not do this."

Marta was right. Chelle worked out with our young group because there simply was no other place to put her. She was the same inconsistent and moody gymnast as before. The time we spent dealing with Chelle's tantrums and problems took time away from the pumpkins.

I had great expectations for Amanda Uherek. She was a small child, very similar in body type to Nadia. I suspected that she would grow into the same powerful body type and exhibit a grace similar to Nadia's. Amanda was an excellent performer—God, she was good! She could do much more in the competitions than she could do in her workouts. A strong mind, that one, a very strong mind.

Erica Stokes was a supercoordinated young girl who was discovered, like most of the others, at the camps we hold over the summer. Erica and her parents moved from Kansas to join our club. Erica quickly excelled on the beam and the floor.

Amy Scheer did not have a very stable competitive approach. She was pretty breakable during competitions, but she was a hard worker and a positive influence on the team. Amy always pushed herself beyond her limits. One more time, one more time, she always said. Amy never said no, and she never abandoned an event before she made a final attempt to get everything out of it.

Hilary Grivich was the youngest in the group. Her unique consistency made her invaluable. She was unshakable, super confident, and extremely consistent.

Kerri Strug's gymnastic abilities were excellent as a result of her natural speed and coordination. Her level of difficulty on each apparatus was remarkable. She was an asset to the team, and a highly impressive gymnast.

It is difficult to tell, with children who are nine, ten, and eleven, who will become a champion. You can tell how flexible they are, how coordinated, but not if they have the spirit, or if they can develop the mental and physical discipline necessary to become a superstar.

At the beginning, it didn't look like Kim Zmeskal would develop into a great gymnast. The only thing evident to me at the outset of her career was her natural speed. Her little legs could move so fast that her heels looked like a blur as they pumped up and down. When she ran toward the horse her speed was incredible. I used to joke with Mary Lou, "Look at your little sister over there." Kim was just as round and neat as Mary Lou had been. However, at the beginning of her career, Kimbo was legendary for different reasons.

Kim Zmeskal was legendary for her falls. She'd fall regularly from the beam during a routine. She was like popcorn popping on and off. And most of the time she'd mess up her floor routines by over-rotating her somersaults. And there was something else about Kim, which Marta noticed.

"Bela," Marta said one afternoon, "have you noticed that as soon as you step into the gym, the first one to jump up to an event and do something more than she has ever done before is Kim?" I started to pay a little more attention to Kim. It was true, Kim was the one who was seeking the attention. She was a performer under the watching eye of the people she considered important. Her mind was set like a computer.

In 1989, the team was ready for its first Junior National competition. The kids had begun to perform consistently. To our surprise, Kim won the all-around competition and began to distinguish herself as the leading personality of the group.

Following the Junior Nationals I received a call from Mrs. Okino about her daughter Betty. She was a Rumanian living in Chicago, and she wanted her daughter to come and train with me. I told her that we already had a set team, even though Chelle Stack's position was always in question. Mrs. Okino kept calling me, and I finally said, "Okay, bring her down and whatever happens will happen."

Mrs. Okino entered the gym with two little black girls. She was white, very Rumanian-looking, and I asked her where her daughter was. Betty stepped forward and said, "I'm right here." Oh, my goodness, I felt silly. After Betty went to warm-up, Marta pulled me aside. "That's the one," she said to me, "the kid I noticed at the Nationals."

Betty's mother left shortly after Betty arrived, and her grandmother, who was from Transylvania, came to stay with Betty. Workouts proceeded well, and Betty began to fit in with the group. As usual, Marta and I discussed the kids' workouts in Rumanian when we saw mistakes or flaws that we didn't feel like mentioning. Then we began to notice something strange. Whenever we commented in Rumanian about things that the kids should have done better, the correction was there in their next routine.

One day Marta and I said something about Betty. You should have seen her eyes—they got so huge and round. Holy cow! "Betty, come over here," I said. "You know Rumanian, don't you?" "Yes," she whispered. All those months and months Betty had been telling the kids everything we said. We had a big laugh—then we switched to Hungarian.

Betty was a lovely child, a great personality. Her body type was long and lean, compared to the six pumpkins, and she presented a totally different performance. Her progress was extremely rapid, and she quickly moved to the second position on the team—right behind Kim.

In 1990, the team moved full force toward the American Cup. This is one of the most prestigious competitions in the United States, and almost the most prestigious in the world. Nadia was the first American Cup Champion in 1976. Mary Lou won it for three consecutive years. Kristie and Phoebe also won the Cup.

As had happened several times in the past, we went to the American Cup with a little itty-bitty kid, Kim, as our contender. And that child dazzled everybody, I mean everyone! Kim swept the all-around with a sensational performance, and in the process became the leading gymnast in America. She was fantastic. The sensation of a young unknown child once again defeating the big names. We headed for the Grand Prix.

The Grand Prix is a competition held in Paris. Every major competitor from every major country is there. Kim swept the all-around and established her name in the international arena. We returned to the United States and swept the Senior National Championships. Then we went to the 1990 Olympic Sports Festival. We took six of the first seven places and Kim once again prevailed.

We returned to Houston, Texas, and began our push before the 1990 Goodwill Games—an important international competition that begins to set the reputations and status of gymnasts prior to the Olympic Games. Our team's work ethic and their workouts had to move to a higher level if we hoped to successfully compete against the Rumanians and the Soviets in the Games.

I held a meeting. "We can no longer afford to. be even the slightest bit lazy," I began. "You must be willing to put in sturdy and solid performances day after day based on your individual and unique capabilities—do not copy each other. You must pay attention and focus on your own goals. There will be no individual attention paid to those who waste time. You know your own capabilities and I expect you to perform at your highest level. Lowering your standards will lower the quality of your performances, and I know you do not want that. No more compromising." The kids responded.

We headed to the Goodwill Games.

In Rumania, we grew up with a very strong sense of our patriotic duty. It was my duty to represent my country, to represent the kids, and to make sure that no one ever hurt those kids. Rumania, and my life there as a coach, was full of politics and back-stabbing, egomaniacs, and narrow-minded, self-motivated men, but no one, and I mean no one, would have ever purposely hurt the gymnasts on the Rumanian team. If anyone hurt the kids, we would reach as one man and get that person. The Rumanian gymnasts were a national treasure, the pride of the country, and they were treated accordingly.

The 1990 Goodwill Games are a painful memory, fraught with snake bites. We were a young team, and we were excited at the opportunity of competing. Throughout the competition, our performances were strong. And although Kim, being injured, had made a slight mistake, Betty stood a good chance of winning the title.

Betty's last event was the vault. We stood waiting for her to be called to begin. The vaulting judges were all talking, and I waved at the Bulgarian judge and signaled that Betty was ready. The Bulgarian judge was an experienced international judge, a lady with a good international reputation. She made a sign for Betty to come to the vault. The judges all turned to watch. .

Betty raced toward the vault, flew through the air, and *puck*, she stuck her landing. We were in seventh heaven. Betty had won the all-round; there was no way that her vault could be scored lower than a 9.95. The judges began to compile their scores. That's when an American judge, Audrey Schweyer, left her position as a judge for the bars and raced over to the judges' panel for the vault.

She protested. Audrey Schweyer, an American, a judge for the bars not the vault, left her position and protested against her own country's gymnast. The vault, she claimed, was not valid because the green light had not been on at the start of the vault. The Bulgarian judge said, "Wait a minute, I gave the sign to commence." "No, no," Schweyer screamed. *"There was no green light!"* The controversy raged for several minutes. The whole time the Bulgarian judge defended us. Defended us against our own countryman.

In the end, Audrey Schweyer succeeded. Betty's vault was thrown out, and she was awarded two more vaults. Marta and I just looked at each other. We could not believe what had happened;

we were in the wrong place. Betty's concentration was shot. Her first (second) vault was a little bit short and she received a 9.65; her second (third) vault was better, but she didn't stick it—9.7. She went from being first in the all-around to fourth place.

I couldn't understand. Audrey Schweyer didn't even have one of her club's gymnasts in the competition. She wasn't fighting for her kids, she was just fighting against mine. Schweyer was fighting against her own country in an international competition! I can understand people like Ellen Berger. They stand up beside their athletes. They are biased, but they are acting solely for their country and for their kids. But I'll never understand Audrey Schweyer.

When we came to the United States we exchanged our Rumanian nationalism for American nationalism. I was determined to fight for my new country just as I had fought for my old one. I knew that everyone was suspicious of me in the '84 Olympics. Suspicious of how I was going to act when my kids faced my former team. But it was clear in my mind. I was representing my new country and new kids. While I was proud of the Rumanian team, I was unquestionably loyal to the American kids who were competing at the time.

I thought that the response I received from my fellow American coaches and the U.S. Gymnastics Federation would have been the same as from the Rumanian coaches and Federation. That perhaps they wouldn't like me, but that they would be proud of the kids. Proud that those kids were winners. What happened at the Goodwill Games tore us apart; it tore at our confidence and it tore at our hearts.

Still, I shouldn't have been surprised. I had seen this before. In 1985, at the last American Cup that Mary Lou Retton competed in following the Olympic Games, Schweyer seemed to be biased against the U.S. Olympic gold medalist. Throughout the competition, Mary Lou gave strong performances in each event, including a memorable and beautiful floor routine. She was winning the competition when Schweyer claimed that she had seen Mary Lou step out of the boundaries during her floor routine. She demanded a deduction of Mary Lou's score.

Mary Lou and a Russian gymnast were fighting for the all-around title. A deduction of her score might have placed Mary Lou second. Luckily, there was enough distance between the two gymnasts' scores that the deduction made no difference. Mary Lou went on to win her third, final, and unprecedented, American Cup victory.

I left the Goodwill Games with an age-old sense of frustration and a growing feeling that I was getting tired of fighting the same old windmills. For the first time in my life, I began to question the fight.

But there was no time to reevaluate. The 1991 American Cup followed at the heels of the Goodwill Games. Up until the American Cup, Kim Zmeskal had not lost a major competition in almost two years. However, a momentary change was in the air. Betty Okino was hot. The 1991 American Cup was spectacular, because two of our gymnasts, Kim and Betty, fought for the all-around title. They fought neck and neck. After a minor mistake on the beam, Betty moved ahead of Kim. Kim then came back with two perfect 10's, one on the floor and one on the vault. They weren't enough.

Betty's final event was the vault. When Betty first came to our club her vaults were terrible. By 1991, however, they had become more than adequate. At the American Cup, Betty surprised us all by receiving a 10 on her vault, and Kim could not make up the difference. In the end, Betty became the American Cup Champion. She also broke Nadia's all-time Cup record.

As always, Kim had fought until the last moment. She was a very interesting performer. She never turned around halfway through a competition and declared victory or defeat. It didn't matter if she was leading by a landslide or on her backside. And if she was losing, she never accepted the situation. Kim would always try to turn a loss around; she would always continue to fight. The reality of a scoring situation never mattered to her.

We took the team to Europe for the German Federation Cup (the DTB Cup). That was a huge international competition held both in Switzerland and in Germany. Kim completed the competition as the all-around champion, but that wasn't the most remarkable event that took place. What stood out was the attitude of Ellen Berger.

Betty Okino was on the bars. Following her routine, her score, a 9.85, flashed across the board. I was satisfied with the score; I had no problem with it—it was decent. I looked up and saw Ellen Berger racing over to the jury table like a tornado. "Oh, God," I moaned, "not that damn woman again." I waited to see if Berger was going to lower Betty's score—the score had placed Betty in the leading position. I was ready to fight. When a new score was raised I was speechless. A 9.9 had replaced Betty's 9.85! Ellen Berger had raised one of my gymnasts' score! Then she came over to me.

"Bela," Ellen Berger began, "I have never seen so elegant or so beautiful a gymnast as Betty Okino." Those were the only good words I had ever heard from Berger's mouth. She turned and walked away. It was unbelievable, but I understood. Ellen Berger, like all those old ladies on the judges panel, dreamed about the old days, the old style of gymnastics. She longed for tall, long, lean gymnasts—she hated the power packs. Betty Okino had reminded Berger of the elegant gymnasts of old, and she had been moved enough to talk to me and praise one of my gymnasts.

27.

Creating a Champion

The battle to create a gymnastic champion begins long before any competition. Strategy lays the groundwork for a gymnast's training, and if that strategy, which involves both mental and physical factors, is inappropriate or inefficient, a gymnast will not succeed regardless of her talent.

I begin a rising group of gymnasts with a four-year plan. In those four years there are seven or eight major goals, but all activity works toward one pinnacle—the Olympic Games. The first year the goal may be the National Championship at the junior level. The next year it may be the Nationals and some European meets, if the kids are ready. The third year includes the Senior Nationals and several international championships, including the World Championship. The fourth year, the Nationals, the Olympic Trials, and finally the Olympic Games.

From the four-year plan, there is yearly preparation. There are three major periods of each year: the preparation, the precompetitive season, and the competitive season. The preparation phase involves strong physical preparation—a charging up of the batteries. During this phase, our gymnasts develop their flexibility, strength, and endurance along with technical skills and new stunts.

The precompetitive season is used to mold individual skills into routines. After the kids have their routines down, approximately ten days before the competitive season begins, we have in-house competitions to help them gain some confidence. No spectators, no parents, nobody in the gym but the coaches and the kids. We make sure that we create competitive excitement, and we award prizes and medals.

After a few competitions within the club, we take our little group to a local club—it doesn't matter if it's next door—so that they can have a competition in a foreign environment. We make sure that we pick a club that will give them good competition, but where they will have their first outside winning satisfaction. We don't take them somewhere to get beaten and come home with their spirits down. The point is to give them their first real shot of confidence. We also identify their weaknesses and make corrections, as well as make any final changes to their routines.

Following this, we take the kids to their first official competition. Usually it's regionally organized, and the kids face real competitive requirements and tougher competition. Then I take them to one more club competition, where I know the equipment is good, the other team is decent, and my kids will win. It's important to give them one final boost before the major competitions begin. Then it's time to compete for real.

The competitive season begins when we have finished our preparation and the build-up of the precompetitive season. By that time the minds and bodies are prepared. The competitive season is broken into two parts—spring and early summer, and then the fall. Between each season the schedule of preparation, precompetition, and competition is repeated.

Each yearly schedule is broken down into a weekly regimen. Every week is a cycle. I am a believer in the human biocycle. After observing the kids, I know that they have a set weekly pattern. Their energy and concentration peak on Fridays and Saturdays, and Sundays and Mondays they're at their lowest. From this pattern, we organize our weekly workouts.

On Monday we concentrate on physical preparation, flexibility exercises, dynamic exercises, races, high intensity, and strong motivation. It is also weight-training day. We don't expect anything from the kids on Mondays, other than a flat workout with no major results.

Tuesday the kids begin to build up. Their stamina and concentration are not strong yet, so the coaches offer a lot of physical help and are very involved in each practice routine. On Tuesday we secure each area or apparatus with crash mats to make the conditions easier and safer for the kids.

Wednesday is a good day. We focus on partial and some full routines, and on concentration and stamina. By Thursday the kids are completing routines, correcting mistakes, and their attention and levels of capability are high.

Friday is the most important day. Whatever new skills the kids need to learn, whatever routines need to be finalized, are brought out on that day. Friday is the most successful day for physical performances and establishing and firming new skills. Saturday is a maintenance day—usually the highs from Friday can be maintained, and practice is strong.

By Sunday the kids' attention levels are low, their physical potential weakens, and their performances lack explosive qualities. If they want a day off, that's the best time. If, however, they don't want a break, if they want to work seven days a week, then we do something other than gymnastics during practice. Sometimes we play soccer, have rope climbing competitions, play basketball— anything that is physical but not gymnastic.

Typical practices last four and a half hours. We used to have three-hour practices, but beginning with Mary Lou's generation I introduced morning conditioning workouts. We simply didn't have enough time in the afternoons for conditioning, and because of the revolution of gymnastics, the high difficulty skills and increased complexity, we needed more time to work on different stunts and movements. The results of the increased workout have been positive. The more hours there are to learn and accumulate, the better a gymnast will perform.

Intensive preparation not only increases a gymnast's level of performance, it helps to eliminate the risk of injuries. Gymnastics is an impact sport with direct contact with the apparatus and floor. Ankles, knees, and wrists are the three major areas where all landing or taking off is generated. Tendonitis, sprains, and stress fractures are the most common injuries. Knee injuries are also fairly common. But 90 percent of all problems can be avoided by developing strength, conditioning, and physical abilities.

It is more difficult to avoid the problem of eating disorders than the problem of injuries in gymnastics. While I don't think the problem is as widespread as the media has tried to show, I have known a handful of gymnasts over the last thirteen years with eating disorders. They were fairly easy to spot—wide eyes, dizziness, and muscle contractions and muscle pain due to the elimination of salt and other natural minerals from the body. I never accused any of them. I would just say, "If you are losing weight by something other than a normal diet, you are doing the worst thing you can do to yourself—you are destroying yourself." Most of the time my warnings worked. If, however, the parents already knew that their child had a disorder, then my speeches weren't successful.

If I couldn't get through to a gymnast, Marta would go to the parents. She would suggest healthy diets and ways to reinforce healthy eating habits. Many times she would succeed, but if the parents themselves had poor dietary habits, then the chance of having them positively influence their kid's habits was small.

Most of the time the parents did know that their child had a problem. Whether they were living their own frustrated athletic careers through their children, or whether they wanted the fame and monetary rewards that a successful gymnast can earn, I don't know. Perhaps they were ashamed. All I know is that there is no reason to allow your child to starve herself.

It's hard for a gymnast when she turns fifteen or sixteen years old and her body begins to change, her hips widen, and she puts on weight without changing her eating habits. When this begins to happen diet is extremely important. It's a critical time when the girl can go either way—fat or thin. It's also the time when the gymnast decides how to handle her weight gain—diet and exercise or throwing up, starving, and taking laxatives.

What gymnasts don't understand is that if they gain weight, not fifty pounds but the natural five or ten that come with puberty, it's not the end of the world. They just have to develop their strength to match that weight. Look at Diane Durham and Mary Lou Retton. Two solid kids, not butterflies, who worked hard to build their strength to match their size.

Part of the problem with the diets of gymnasts is that they are receiving wrong information. The most common: have a huge macaroni and cheese dinner before competition because the carbohydrates will increase your strength and capabilities. *Pah!* I'd like to see who the hell can burn off seven thousand calories—maybe a marathon runner, but not a fourteen-year-old kid. If you can't work off a meal, then you will gain weight and get bigger and bigger. Gymnasts must eat well-balanced meals of fruits, vegetables, fish, and meat. Yes, meat.

I have always considered the elimination of meat from the diet as terribly wrong. Meat is a protein that sticks in your stomach for a long time, eliminates the hunger sensation, and slowly releases energy. When I first began coaching in Onesti, I had to decide what types of meals we'd serve Nadia's bunch. I looked at the animals in the animal kingdom, and I thought to myself, Look at the tigers, they are strong, aggressive, quick, and explosive—exactly what I want my gymnasts to be. Look at the cow eating only grass . . . *moo.* I decided that my kids would have the same fuel that the tiger had.

We fed Nadia's generation steaks four or five times a week. The rest of the week they got grilled chicken or fish. In addition, they could have all the salad and fruit they wanted. At one point we cut down on the meat, and the effects were unbelievable. They gained an average of five pounds each week! We went back to meat.

Calcium must also be a part of a gymnast's diet. Cauliflower or broccoli will never supply enough calcium. Kids must drink milk and eat cheese. With Nadia's group we made them eat cheese every morning—they hated it, but it was important. We also filled the water jars in the gym with cold milk so they could sip during workouts.

It was easier back then, because we could control the kids' meals. In America, it is up to their parents, and unfortunately many don't do a good job. We can train our gymnasts to be strong physical and mental competitors. We can give them the gift of self-discipline and confidence, and proven preparation techniques, but we can't make them eat their meat and vegetables. Without the proper fuel, combined with the appropriate preparation, gymnasts are defeated before they begin.

28.

Strategy

I n 1991 I finally had the opportunity to show the American Gymnastic Federation the importance of strategy and timing. I consider the 1991 World Championship one of my greatest strategic coaching successes. I also consider that championship as one of the finest hours of American gymnastics, as the 1991 Worlds were held on American soil, in Indianapolis, home to the U.S. Gymnastics Federation and its President, Mike Jacki.

As I have said, Mike Jacki was famous for avoiding controversial issues. However, through the years he did at times, defend me against the unfair treatment of other coaches. But he never developed too personal a relationship with me. I was a controversial coach and he didn't want to create complications or deeply involve himself in any controversy. However, Jacki was a strong administrator and a great public speaker. He had recently been elected vice president of the International Gymnastic Federation with the realistic opportunity to become the president of that Federation. Jacki was proud of his involvement in the international gymnastics forum, and wanted the 1991 World Championship to be the greatest ever. He had the executive power and the desire to make this goal a reality, but little control over the American athletes' results, which were necessary for his overall success. I was not surprised when he called me for advice on how to turn the U.S. athletes' participation into a major success. Jacki was aware that I was capable of making champions, and I had proven that my capabilities involved a large amount of savvy and strategy. That was exactly what Mike wanted.

Mike flew down to Houston. We talked at length, and he asked me to develop plans for the U.S. Gymnastic Team selection. It was the first time I was given the opportunity to discuss my thoughts on the problems in American gymnastics, specifically in the team selection process for international championships. Mike was receptive as I shared my ideas.

Timing is everything, I told Mike. For prior championships, the Federation held trials months before the actual competitions. That was wrong. It was impossible to evaluate a gymnast's value as a team member when we went for several months without seeing her perform. In four months a fifteen-year-old gymnast can go through massive changes, and her physical and mental status can change dramatically. I told Mike that we should hold trials for the World Championship two weeks before the actual competition. Last moment criteria are the only criteria that matter. By changing the trial date, we would, for the first time, be able to effectively evaluate the readiness of our gymnasts right before the competition.

The right strategic placement of gymnasts for a competition is also vital for success. The opener must be a team player, the clincher must be a sure bet, and there is always a weak performer in each event who must be hidden in the middle of the group. That's how we can get the most out of the team, and the most out of each individual performer, I told Mike. I also said that the U.S. World Championship coach had to evaluate each gymnast's strengths and weaknesses and place each gymnast in the competition accordingly. Then, Mike and I talked about all my other thoughts regarding tactics and strategy. I stressed that the success of our athletes depended not just on their performances, but on the strategical moves made before and during the competition. Mike agreed with all my suggestions, including the selection of the judges for the event.

After Mike accepted my plan, he presented it to the executive committee of the Federation with the request that it be accepted immediately, and that I be named head coach for the World Championship. The executive committee agreed.

I picked an aggressive team—Kim, Betty, Hilary, and Kerri, along with two gymnasts from other clubs, Shannon Miller and Michelle Campi. They were all hungry to succeed. My team was young and relatively unknown—they had nothing to lose. Following the trial, I spent two weeks assessing strengths and weaknesses, and molding the kids into a team.

Forty thousand people packed the Indianapolis arena for the World Championships. The previous world champion, the Soviet Boginskaia, was competing and was in great shape. The Rumanians were there, and they had a burning desire to defeat the Soviets. And the American team, which had no impressive international track record in the World Championship, were there to give the leading gymnasts a run for their money. We had the power, the level of difficulty, the capability, and most important, the guts to go for it.

A new format for the compulsories was introduced that year. Instead of having a team compulsory performance, the gymnasts from each team were divided into three groups of two. Each group competed against the twosomes of other countries in one of four rounds. Which country competed in each round was decided at random. Each team could choose which of their two gymnasts would compete in each round. Each twosome could compete in only one round. We were scheduled to compete in rounds two, three, and four.

Just as in any competition, the scores of the last performers are built upon the success of the first competitors. If our first twosome didn't achieve scores that equaled or exceeded their competitors, then our last twosome would have no hope to make up the difference. They couldn't build on low scores. We would lose in the first round if we didn't achieve higher scores than the rest.

Every country used the same strategy that they had in previous team compulsory competitions. Their openers were their most consistent team members—not the best, but the ones who made no mistakes and could guarantee a decent score. Their next two performers were their stronger gymnasts, and their final two were their stars. How in the world, I asked myself, can I use the new format to defeat our opponents? And then I knew what we had to do—we had to reverse our strategy.

Kerri and Hilary became our openers. They were very strong, confident gymnasts, and their performances were superior to the openers from Rumania and the Soviet Union. Our opening scores were high. Kim and Betty, our two strongest performers, performed in the next round and elevated our team compulsory score, which placed us in front of the Rumanians, the current world champions. Everyone was shocked. I placed Shannon and Michelle, less known but solid performers, in the fourth and final round. All they had to do was put in consistent performances. They did, and they received equally high scores as the big-name gymnasts placed in the final round. The Rumanians, who had saved their best gymnasts for last, had no chance to make up the difference.

The Rumanians went nuts. They were powerful compulsory performers, and had much more competitive experience than our girls. They couldn't understand how a young and inexperienced team had beaten them. The strategy had worked.

We went into the optionals and my little guys were like tigers, jumping and fighting, their spirits boiling. I had them in my hand, and I felt their paws and heard them growl. Our fighting style was just like back in '76—let's go get 'em. The crowd showed their appreciation, cheering like they were at a basketball game.

When the competition ended, for the first time in history, the Americans had defeated the Rumanians' previous world champions. We placed second in the team competition, behind the Soviets. And in another tremendous historical first, Kim Zmeskal won the all-around title. Kim was the first American to ever become an all-around world champion. Her performance during the World Championship was electric—unbelievable power and levels of difficulty performed to perfection. At the time, Kim was only thirteen years old. From that moment on, she was no longer just a person in the sport of gymnastics. Kim became a personality, an idol for millions of little girls, and an impressive part of U.S. gymnastics history.

29.

What Kind of Coyotes Eat Their Own Pups?

I never expected things to go super smooth. The struggle to succeed is part of the sport of gymnastics. I believe very much in the sport, and the value of the struggle . . . as long as the fight is a fair one.

We had faced the fierce competition of the Rumanians and Soviets at the 1991 World Championship, and we had been victorious. The result was that Kim Zmeskal became a national idol, a role model, a powerful symbol of a young athlete who could succeed, pass any difficulties, and beat the best athletes in the world through a disciplined, organized, dedicated life.

Early in 1992 we received information about the first individual World Championship, to be held in Paris, France, the heart of Europe. The competition did not fit into our preparation plan, but I still decided to go, recognizing the importance of the competition for the outcome of the Olympic Games. The world needed to see that Kim wasn't the World Champion because of the home-court advantage, but her own skill and athletic prowess. In addition, I felt it was important to have one more successful European competition in a country next door to Barcelona—where the Games were to be held.

The first individual World Championship was a great success for Kim Zmeskal. Kim became the World Champion on the beam and floor. Her dynamic, spectacular, and technically superior floor exercise—performed to the American rock and roll tune "Rock Around the Clock"—was the highlight of the competition. Kim's floor routine was another great choreographic creation by Geza Pozsar, my dear friend, who through the years choreographed hundreds of floor routines, many of which were presented by our gymnasts in winning performances in European, World, and Olympic Games. There is no doubt, besides the memorable floor routines performed by Nadia and Mary Lou, that Kim's 1992 floor routine was one of the best ever choreographed and performed. Betty Okino also had an excellent performance, becoming the silver medalist on the uneven bars and performing her unique triple pirouette on the beam—named "the Okino."

When we returned from Paris, we wasted no time before beginning to prepare for upcoming Olympic events. I did not expect much of a fight at the 1992 U.S. Senior National Championship. I expected the appreciation of our accomplishments to be reflected in the crowd's enthusiasm and the judges' scores.

We had three gymnasts in the Nationals who had been the backbone of the World Championship team. Kim, Hilary, and Kerri (Betty Okino was injured and could not compete) had earned their rankings as the top gymnasts in the world. They had earned the right to expect appreciation from their country. Yet that was not the case. Some of the judges at the 1992 Senior Nationals were club affiliated, with their own agendas. That left only a minority of fair and objective judges on the floor. Facing this unexpected reality was a painful experience, difficult to understand, and confusing for the participating athletes.

To try to discredit Kim two months before the Olympic Games was stupid and unbelievably cruel. She wasn't just a person in gymnastics, she was a personality who elevated the whole sport of American gymnastics. She should have been protected, cherished, and preserved.

When Nadia became a champion, nobody, no matter what, would ever have done a thing to discredit or hurt her. She was the pride of the nation. Kim Zmeskal was also an idol. Her country had a patriotic duty to protect her. When a gymnast gives so much joy and pride to her country, the least she can expect in return is fairness.

Then there was Hilary Grivich, the one who, as our opener, helped us to place second as a team in the World Championship. The one who had the personality, the confidence, the calm, and the ability to avoid mistakes and produce consistent and strong performances. Hilary was singled out by certain National Championship judges in an attempt to eliminate her. Why Hilary? Because they couldn't really destroy Kim, she was too good, or Betty, who was injured, or Kerri, whose levels of difficulty were outstanding.

Throughout the Nationals, Hilary's scores were cut—points deducted for imaginary mistakes or for slight imperfections overlooked in other gymnasts. She ended up placing eighth. Thirty percent of her score, as with all the gymnasts, would be added to her Olympic Trials score to determine the Olympic team. Hilary's chances were crippled. I knew Hilary would eventually be eliminated.

I protested. Immediately after the Nationals I called Mike Jacki and tried to arrange a meeting. I wanted to explain to him that the judging, which had solely represented club interests, was going to have a disastrous effect on the selection of the Olympic team. Club-affiliated judges had no place at the Nationals or the Olympic Trials.

I wanted to tell him that we were creating our own monster. That monster was going to chase us, and we would bleed to death. Mike promised me that we would meet, but that meeting never took place. I believe he simply didn't want to become part of the brewing controversy.

The monster came out of the woods at the 1992 Olympic Trials. The club-affiliated judges had organized themselves further. The Trials were a nightmare for Hilary and Kim. It was paralyzing and shocking to many that American judges would eliminate two kids who would have been an asset to the Olympic team. Event after event the kids were hammered. Kerri escaped only because the judges were focusing on eliminating our strongest and weakest. Betty did not compete because she was still injured.

I tried to get Mike to intervene. "A disaster is developing on the floor which is our disaster, nobody else's," I explained. "The international gymnastics community is going to laugh at us, because we destroyed our own capabilities, our own potential." Finally Mike tried to intervene, giving out warnings for biased judgings to Schweyer's bunch, but it was too late. The big ball was rolling.

Hilary was eliminated. And in a move that would ultimately contribute to the breaking of Kim's spirit, she won the Trials but was still placed second behind Shannon Miller. Kim Zmeskal had won both the Trials and the Nationals. Shannon Miller, who had not completed the National competition due to injury was scored solely on her performance at the Trials. The original selection process of combined scoring—70 percent from the Trials, 30 percent from the Nationals, was discarded in Miller's case. Therefore, even though Kim won the Trials, based on her all-around score, only 70 percent of that score counted toward her final combined score. One hundred percent of Miller's Trials score was counted. Based on that scoring system, Shannon was placed first, even though based on the Trials scores Kim had won. Even more ludicrous was the fact that Shannon, having missed competing in the National competition, could not, by the Federation's own rules, be named the winner of the Trials regardless of her performance. Miller was petitioned into the Trials and based on her all-around performance, second to Kim's, she was qualified to be part of the Olympic team, but she could not be ranked at that point because she had not participated in the Nationals. That fact was never fully explained to the media.

"Wait a minute," I screamed. Nobody listened; nobody from the Federation stepped in and said that there was a error that needed to be corrected. Nobody explained to the media that Kim Zmeskal was really the winner of the Trials. And nobody defended the National and World Champion. I asked for an explanation of the judging but nobody could give me one. There was no way to explain that type of ruling. Then the next issue emerged—the injured gymnasts—the ones who had not been able to compete either at the Nationals or the Trials. "What about Betty Okino, how are we going to figure out whether she should be on the Olympic team," the Federation people asked. Their solution? Another Trial.

Another Trial? Betty was my own athlete, and my heart was for her, my blood was pumping for her, but another Trial? It wasn't fair to the kids who had been eliminated, like Grivich, to have another Trial without giving them an opportunity to secure a position. I wanted Betty on the team more than anyone else, but another Trial was unfair and I said so.

No one listened. I knew in my heart that the next Trial wasn't even for Betty. The additional Trial was renamed a "Trial to select a training squad for the Olympics." And the ensuing Trial was called the "intersquad training meet for final Olympic team selections."

The gymnasts who had placed in the top six places in the original Trial were lined up for the second Trial. Betty Okino, Michelle Campi, and Wendy Bruce, from Brown's gymnastics, were added to the group. The Trial, or rather the intersquad meet, was designated to held at Brown's club. "How in the world," I asked, "can we have a fair trial at a private gym? Put it on the moon, put it in the dirtiest little village in the world, put it in the desert, but not in a private club that has an athlete in the Trial. That gives the athlete an unfair home-court advantage.

The monster was getting bigger and uglier. There was no shrinking from it anymore, no chance of defeating it. The only way to go was to make more mistakes. All previous scores were wiped clean, and based on the judging controversies in the previous trial, a decision was made that the judges for the final Trial would be the coaches. Can you believe it? Private, individual coaches whose athletes were on the floor were the judges. Couldn't we find, in the entire U.S., four unbiased, competent judges to officiate an Olympic Trial? There were no scores. The kids performed their routines, and when they finished, the coaches voted. Kids were chosen by votes, not by scores that determined the levels of difficulty, mistakes, strengths, and weaknesses, but by votes.

Kim Kelly was eliminated. There was no doubt that she was the weakest of the group. Her elimination, however, couldn't bring back a Grivich, or any of the other strong athletes who had been eliminated in the first two competitions. In the end, three of my kids—Kim, Kerri, and Betty—made the team. Shannon Miller, Dominique Dawes, and Wendy Bruce were also named Olympic team members. Of the three, I was happy to see Shannon Miller on the team. She was a strong and talented gymnast and deserved her spot. But there was no way that a strong, unified Olympic team could be formed from those kids. Their unity had been ripped to pieces by the sorry experience of the biased selection procedure. A team spirit could not be built upon such a controversial foundation.

The media didn't help the situation. Shannon Miller and Kim, members of the same Olympic team, were portrayed by the media as enemies. Journalists, intent only on selling papers, wrote false stories to create controversy instead of positive stories that would boost the morale of the team. Shannon and Kim were not from the same club, but they weren't enemies. Personally, I was excited to have Shannon on the team. She was a good athlete and I was proud of her accomplishments. She would give us a better chance to fight for individual and team performances. Why couldn't the media see that?

All I saw was the devastating effects the Trials had on the athletes. All the athletes, not just my own. I saw gymnasts question their value, and their place on the Olympic team, and I saw gymnasts who truly belonged on the team, those who had been eliminated, question their years of dedication and training. It was a sad situation. Many people think the stress and strain on young gymnasts to practice and compete is too much. The practices and the competitions aren't the problem. Young gymnasts can handle long workouts and defeat at the hands of a competitor. Those events give kids discipline and confidence, as well as an understanding of themselves and their abilities. What they cannot emotionally handle, and should not have to handle, is the self-motivated cruel actions of adults involved in the sport. It's the blatant cheating, manipulations, and dishonesty that break a child's spirit.

Kim Zmeskal's spirit was systematically broken. It began with the Nationals. I could see it in her eyes—they were wide open, trying to understand some of the judges. I could see that her mind was full of confusion. Am I the one who is supposed to be appreciated? Or, am I a public enemy? Who am I? What is this situation? What is going on here? Why do these people hate me? Kim had just won the World Championship, she had the right to expect appreciation. All I could say to Kimbo throughout the whole mess was be strong. But that wasn't enough. She wasn't one to be fooled by a pat on the back. She knew what was going on, and she knew it would only get worse.

What kind of coyotes eat their own pups?

30.

Olympic Magic

I remember Olympic Villages that were magical. I recall a spirit of mutual admiration and a unique level of communication, despite language barriers. Hands would fly, bodies would dance, and songs and jokes would make the village electric with music and laughter. Everyone inside the village was a nonprofessional athlete with the same goal: glory for themselves and their country.

That was before Dream Teams, cereal box contracts, and million-dollar endorsements. That was before professional athletes, and the politicians and avaricious businessmen that promoted them, were allowed to enter the Olympic Games. The Olympics have always been the pinnacle for amateur athletes. Now, for example, we must tell young athletes who have worked all their lives to play basketball that they must first join a professional basketball team and secure a multimillion-dollar contract to have a chance to become an Olympian. The time of innocent amateur sports was over.

I am not a dinosaur. I am not alone in my distaste for what the

Olympics have become. The 1992 Olympic Village in Barcelona, Spain, was pervaded by jealousy and suspicion. In the past, all athletes competing in the Games lived in the village. They adhered to strict rules—no drinking, no late-night parties, no male/female fraternizing. In 1992 the rules changed. Professional athletes took rooms in the most exclusive hotels in Spain while amateur athletes stayed in the village's dorms. For the first time, living in those dorms did not feel like the honor it was. Then there were the parties. Every night I had to ask athletes in the dorm to be quiet so my gymnasts could sleep. There was no respect for fellow athletes or for the Games.

"What can I get out of this?" seemed to be the new attitude of the athletes in 1992. I can't really blame them. They watched professional athletes arrive at the Games in limousines. They watched the Dream Team get unbelievable press coverage for demolishing amateur teams that were more interested in getting Magic Johnson's autograph than in playing ball. The 1992 Olympics taught amateur athletes one thing: There's money to be made. How do you explain to a fifteen-year-old gymnast, a twenty-year-old swimmer, or a seventeen-year-old diver that distinction and honor for herself and her country are more important than a $3 million endorsement from a bottled-water company?

Politics and money are the driving forces in athletics. Perhaps they were all along, and I just refused to admit their overwhelming strength. Perhaps I have fought all my life for a type of purity that doesn't really exist. The 1992 Olympic Games convinced me that until the U.S. Gymnastics Federation and Olympic Committee make a commitment to fight for that purity, and for the success of their athletes, regardless of who the coaches are, I can no longer fight alone. I am tired.

I was tired when we arrived in Barcelona with a team composed of individual gymnasts—some broken, some unsure of their value, some happy only to have reached the Games and uncaring about their final performance.

They were a group of kids with no faith in themselves. Nothing I said could make them gain the electricity and excitement so vital to charge them before the Games. Every morning I reminded them that the next few days would be the most memorable moments of their lives, but nobody believed my words—not even me.

Those kids had been damaged. The Trials had left them with the feeling that perhaps someone else deserved their spot. There was no fighting spirit, no take 'em dead or alive attitude. There were just six separate kids with separate coaches training for the Games.

From the beginning, we didn't have a good start. The compulsories began with a shaky opener—we were missing a consistent one like Grivich. Our opener's performance affected the team, placing us behind the Russians and Rumanians. Still, we received fairly high scores based on the past prestige of the American team. The international gymnastics judging community had expected an equally strong showing in the '92 Games as we'd had in the 1991 World Championships. By the second day of the competition the judges figured out that we were no longer that strong, and our scores reflected that perception.

Our scores also reflected the American judges' lack of understanding of international judging. Throughout the competition, American judges scored their own athletes lower than any other judges. They called their judging fair; I call it stupid.

I want to make it clear that I believe in fairness. I do not want anything undeserved for myself or my gymnasts. But there are factors in judging that need to be taken into account. In international judging, there must be a rebalancing of the judging average by different countries. I am not talking about cheating, I'm talking about recognizing an established system where individual countries favor their own gymnasts. If our judges do the same, then the total comes out even, and all gymnasts compete on equal footing.

International scoring has always been this way. It is reasonable to say it will not change any time soon. As long as the judges from each country enter a competition with a good understanding of the system, and a strong sense of patriotism, a balance is struck. There is no room for idealistic judges in the international gymnastics arena. Fair judges, yes, but fair judges recognize that the international scoring system has not changed for thirty years, and if they want each gymnast to have an equal opportunity for success they must face reality. I appreciate everyone; I also appreciate my own athletes—that's what I've always understood the system to be based on. American judges have yet to grasp this principle. It seems so strange that something I find so obvious eludes them. Perhaps it is because I am not idealistic.

After months of being hammered into the dirt, Kim understood not only the fatal flaw in American judging, but the fact that many U.S. judges did not value or support her. During the Games, I saw her gaze wander around the arena, and I wanted to just shake her and say that everything up until that point had been a bad dream. I could not do that much lying. I could not tell her that everything was rosy. I could not rebuild her spirit.

Of course, the Games went poorly for Kim and Betty. They went into the '92 Olympics not as fighters who were planning to experience a great moment of their gymnastic lives, but to perform the swan song of their athletic careers. It is difficult to fight with fire and aggressiveness when you know you are playing your last chord. They made mistakes that I had never seen before; they had lost their concentration, their ambition, and their drive. They had been broken. They were athletes who had faced a corrupt system for too many months; they were overwhelmed by the negativity, the pettiness, and the cruelty. Those blank looks, strained faces, and tearful eyes the television public saw during the competition were not the result of the pressure of their sport, but the pressure of understanding what was going on, the lack of support of their own judges, and the mind games they had been forced to endure up until the Games.

Young gymnasts who excel, who bring glory to themselves and their countries, expect and deserve appreciation, not a knife in the back.

Immediately after the Games, Kim and Betty left with their parents. They went back to school and to their own private lives. I was not surprised. I took their decision as a part of reality. They had experienced great athletic careers; it was time to go on with their lives. Kerri decided to continue with her gymnastics career.

In the end, the 1992 Olympic Games left a bitter taste in my mouth that I could no longer swallow. It was everything in combination—the judging, the cheating, the Nationals and Trials, the media's method of pushing the sport in the wrong direction, the Federation's apathy, and the little victims. When the Games were over, I walked up to an American judge on the floor who had given our athletes the lowest scores of any country. I said, "You cannot call yourself an American judge, you are just a piece of trash." The beauty of the sport at the elite level had disappeared for me.

Prior to the Olympics, Marta and I had discussed the fact that one day we were going to step back from top-level coaching. For some time, we had felt that American gymnastics was slipping in the wrong direction. A direction we couldn't live with. Until 1992, we believed the fight was worth every minute. That the frustration was worth it, because every time we had a victory we moved forward. Until 1992, we felt that we were adding to the American gymnastics program, and that out of our struggle we were creating individuals who would lead the gymnastics community and elevate the sport to a higher level. After the 1992 Games, I looked around and saw that my frustrations were no longer worth the effort. For the first time I felt an emptiness that could not be filled by returning to the gym to coach the next generation of elite gymnasts.

I decided to step back. I recognized that after twelve years as an American elite coach, the gymnastics community had gotten too used to results. They expected Mary Lou Retton, Kristie Phillips, Phoebe Mills, or Kim Zmeskal to always appear in the Olympic Games. They took the gymnasts for granted. They took my hard work for granted. I was tired of fighting windmills. Despite my frustration, looking back on the past thirty years of coaching, I recognize that I still have to consider myself very fortunate to have been able to spend my entire life doing what I love the most, feel a deep passion for, and what I consider the most beautiful expression of the ultimate in human capabilities—the sport of gymnastics. I realize my frustration has nothing to do with my profession. I still love coaching and being part of the beautiful sport of gymnastics. I simply decided that I needed a change.

I want to make it clear that no one pushed Marta and me out of the sport. It was our own decision to take a break. Perhaps if the American gymnastics community gains a better understanding of how to handle the competitive program and how to preserve the prestige of its athletes, Marta and I will return. For now, however, destiny has turned us in another direction.

During the worst moments of the Games I closed my eyes and tried to remember happier times. The images that flashed in my mind were the little faces of my first gymnasts in Vulcan. Little faces full of joy and gratefulness. After the Games I realized that those images were a call from destiny. Maybe those little ones deserved my attention again. Maybe it was time to shine the light into their lives, to give them a boost, a motivation, and a faith in their own capabilities. Maybe it was time to go back to my roots.

I had always held on to a part of the little ones. Ever since I came to this country I had tried to split my time and effort between working with the elite gymnasts and traveling with gymnastic shows to small towns to work with children. After the Games, I decided that for the first time I would concentrate solely on working with little kids. It is just as prestigious as working for gold medals, and the sense of accomplishment on both sides is just as strong.

Today, we travel around the country doing clinics for children and putting together gymnastic shows with legendary gymnasts like Diane Durham, Nadia Comaneci, Bart Conner, Kim Zmeskal, and Betty Okino. We bring unforgettable moments to thousands of kids. We are doing a great service for the American gymnastics program—more than I could ever do at the top level.

I feel a great sense of fulfillment when I realize that we are working to bring American gymnastics back to reality. Gymnastics doesn't just exist at the top, it begins with the little ones. I teach kids to appreciate gymnastics at the beginning, to not refuse the beginning, and the process of learning and developing skills.

Too many kids walk into a gym and immediately want to become Olympic champions. If the next day they don't do a triple back somersault, they aren't satisfied. Their parents are also impatient and want results, and if they don't see them they take their kid out of the sport. I teach children that anything worthwhile is worth working for. I tell them to enjoy the sport, take the challenges, and be proud of their accomplishments. They must stick with it, be patient, dedicated and disciplined. That is how, someday, they may be in the position of their idols.

Teaching children that gymnastics can give them everything— year after year of satisfaction, physical and emotional strength, a healthy mind and sturdy positive attitude—is my number one priority right now. That is more important to me than fighting at the top and struggling to preserve elite gymnasts whose value is not fully recognized.

31.

Saltomortale

W hen my grandmother was ninety years old she was still stubborn, strong, and hard on me. One day, I came home dead tired from an athletic competition. Before I could sit down to rest, my grandmother sent me to feed the animals and bring water from the well. "Leave me alone," I begged. "I've just spent four hours at a track competition, and there's no way you can understand how tired I am because you've never been involved in sports." My grandmother just looked at me and scoffed. "A competition, big deal. I've never done a competition, that's right, but I've done a *saltomortale* [a somersault]. I did a *saltomortale* when I was fifteen years old, and I didn't even get hurt because I was strong from working in the fields. I could have been in a competition, but they were not in fashion at the time. So get the bucket, Bela, and bring in some water, you big shot."

That night I asked my father when my grandmother had ever done a somersault. My father said that when his mother was a young girl, she had been on top of a hay wagon when the horses got spooked and raced off before she could grab the reins. My grandmother had been thrown backward and, by the grace of God, had done a back flip in the air and landed on her feet. She had done a *saltomortale*.

Whether my grandmother had done a somersault on purpose or not wasn't the point. The point was that after almost eighty years she still felt pride. That somersault had given her confidence a boost that had lasted a lifetime. That's what I do in my summer gymnastic camps. I give kids an opportunity they have dreamed of but might never have had the chance, or the courage, to experience.

Marta and I have been running some type of summer camp ever since we moved to Houston, Texas. At first, we ran traveling camps, like a circus, with equipment that we'd set up and tear down in one day. Those were exhausting sixteen- to eighteen-hour days, and we repeated those days for weeks at a time. Not only did we set up and tear down our traveling gymnasium, we also spent each day spotting hundreds of kids—twisting, lifting, turning, and throwing. At night we were so tired, our fingers jammed and broken, our shoulders aching, but we were happy. There was such satisfaction in working with the little ones.

As our commitment to competitive gymnastics increased, we had to cut back on the traveling camps. But I never gave up the idea that someday I would return to spending most of my time with the camps and the little kids. I realized, after the 1992 Olympic Games, that "someday" had finally come.

By 1985, we had already begun to hold some of our camps in the Houston gym, and a few out on our ranch in New Waverly, Texas. In 1989, we moved the entire operation to the ranch. Today, due to Marta's and my increased involvement, the camp runs from June 15 to August 15—one-week sessions, six hours a day. More than two thousand kids enroll each summer, many for more than one session. The kids live in beautiful cedar log cabins on the ranch, which I built along with three gymnasiums and several other buildings including our own ranch house.

The ranch is set on three hundred acres in the middle of the Sam Houston National Forest. I have fifty head of cattle, thirteen horses, several dogs, a camel named Leroy, two deer named Daisy and Rocky, a llama, miniature donkeys, mules named Samson and Delilah, goats, pigeons, chickens, turkeys, roosters, and raccoons named Rocky and Baby Rambo. The animals are for me, because I have never outgrown my love for nature's creatures, and for the kids. Some of the kids who come to our camp have never seen a cow, let alone a camel. In addition to six hours of intensive gymnastics practice each day, we take them on horseback rides and hay rides, and let them play with all the gentle animals.

My goal is to give our campers an experience they will never forget. In addition to the animals, I have soccer fields, a swimming pool, and tennis courts for them to play on. We also have barbecues, campfires, baseball games, swimming races, and tennis competitions. There are ghost hunts and all the silly, fun games that children love and remember all their lives. In addition, I had a man-made lake bulldozed on my property so that we can have paddle boats and canoes.

We employ more than sixty coaches each summer. That's the largest coaching staff in the whole United States. They are all young people, all excited, all ready to tear down mountains. They put a tremendous effort into the camps, and by the end of each session they are pretty tired and beaten up. Rule number one is that no child must ever crash in the gym. The coaches get black eyes, broken fingers, and bruised ribs, keeping the kids out of danger. But they wouldn't have it any other way.

At the end of each session I remind the coaching staff that all their work will have a tremendous effect on the lives of each child they worked with—a long-term effect. There are also the precious moments that each of the coaches will remember, like when a little kid walks up and hugs and thanks them for helping them learn their first flipflop. Every summer our coaches return for weeks or months of hard work and happiness.

A certain percentage of the kids in our camps will never be involved in daily training once they leave us. Perhaps they won't have the opportunity to go to a gym in their hometown, perhaps their families don't have the money for day-to-day coaching. But for one week those kids are gymnasts. The things they accomplish in our camp will stick with them for their entire lives. Their first somersault will be remembered when they are ninety years old.

I try to impress upon parents the importance of allowing their child to experience a summer of freedom. I tell them not to take away those memories of pillow fights in the cabins, of friendships with kids from across the country, of athletic successes, and campfire songs. Those are the greatest times for children as well as for adults. For adults, summer camp is a moment in their child's life where she is in a controlled, directed, safe environment free of the risks and hazards of the real world. It is a moment to be cherished.

We never had anything like our camp in Rumania. When I first came to the United States and began to work at Paul Ziert's camps, I was so amazed. Here were kids, not elite gymnasts or promising future competitors, experiencing all the positive things that the sport can give. The atmosphere was positive, and the kids were so grateful for the opportunity to experience something they had not experienced before.

I will never forget my first camp experiences in the United States. For Marta and me, the camps were like coming out of a nightmare—seeing the light for the first time since our defection. But more than that, we fell in love with the sense of satisfaction that working with the little ones provides every second of the day.

32.

Peace

Where is my home? Do I miss my native country, my family, my old friends? Do I wonder what my life might have been, could have been . . . should have been?

If I have learned anything the last fifty years, I have learned that there are no "should have beens." Fate has ruled my life. It brought me to America and dictated that I shall not be buried in my native soil, to become a part of the mountains and valleys where generations of Karolyis lie.

I have finally made peace with my past. It was not easy. In May 1993, Marta, Andrea, and I returned, for the first time since our defection, to Rumania. I did not want to go. Friends who had recently visited our native country reported a land torn by poverty and misery. I did not want to see that. And if I am to be completely truthful, I did not want to face the question that has tugged at the corners of my mind for the last twenty-odd years. Would I have found the degree of success, of personal and professional fulfillment, that I have found in the United States had I stayed in Rumania?

The trip to Rumania was wonderful. It wasn't just seeing my parents, it wasn't just visiting my old school in Deva, which still prospers, and it wasn't just introducing Andrea to the people and country she had so little time to know. It was the realization that the people who made the most of life, regardless of their circumstances, were still making the most of life. The miners, the teachers, the farmers, who had been happy and fulfilled in the past, were still just as happy. The ones who had always found something to complain and cry about were still crying. I finally had my answer.

It isn't where you are, or whether you are born the child of a miner or an engineer. The quality of life is determined by individuals, not places or situations. I felt such a sense of peace, knowing, truly knowing, that had I stayed I would have still found happiness, because that is my nature. I will always be a fighter, whether in my new country or my old. And I will always find the bright parts of life, because that is my way.

And it doesn't matter where my home is, or where I will be buried. Yes, I miss the beauty of the Carpathian mountains, the rushing streams, and the wildflowers that carpet the village where I was born. But all I have to do is close my eyes and I can smell the crisp mountain air and hear the bugling of the elk calling me. And in my heart, I can wrap my arms around the places and the people I love, both in America and Rumania, and in doing so, I know that I will always be home.

Index

confidence built in, 37, 79, 218
experience needed for, 78, 83, 171, 199, 210
in four-year plan, 198–99
for Olympic Games preparation, 47, 210
for Olympic team selection, 53–54, 145–49, 171–74, 210–11
and podium workouts, 58, 178–79
and pride, *see* pride
role of opener in, 170–71, 205, 218
timing for, 205
see also specific competitions
compulsories, new (1991) format for, 206–7
Conner, Bart, 106, 116–17, 124, 125, 222
control:
by bureaucracy, 148, 162
by Ceauşescu, 73
by Federation, *see* Rumanian Gymnastics Federation; U.S. Gymnastics Federation
of kids' diets, 203
self-, 35, 37, 70–71, 110, 173, 187, 193
copying, and winning, 46, 141
Crouse, Scott, 143, 145
Cuba:
Friendship Cup in, 78–80
one-way tickets to, 79–81
Czechs, as competitors, 44–45

Davydova, Yelena, 93–95
Dawes, Dominique, 214
defection, 107–15, 118
Deva, Rumania:
gymnastics program in, 75–78, 101–3
homecoming to, 85–86, 228
Nadia in, 84, 85–86
public support in, 76, 101–2
selection process for, 77
diets, of gymnasts, 201–3
Dinamo Sports Club:
Bela disliked by, 56
and European Championship, 49, 51

and Gymnastics Federation, 47
and Olympics, 46–47, 54–56
power and money of, 38, 46–47, 53
dirty tricks:
booing by soldiers, 92–93, 99
and defection, 107–8
for gold, 68
manipulated scoring, 93–95
Nadia's operation, 1, 3, 87
one-way tickets, 79–81, 82
team stolen, 71–74
discipline:
importance of, 35, 37, 110–11, 173, 187, 222
vs. laxity, 70–71, 81, 193
and post-Olympic frenzy, 62–64
in sports, 165, 187–88, 222
Dumitru, Viorica, 43–44
Durham, Diane, 134, 138–49, 202
in 1984 Olympic Trials, 145–49
contribution to gymnastics of, 142
removed from training, 143–44, 145
and sports clinics, 222
technical ability of, 140–41

East Germans, *See* Germans
eating disorders, 201–2
Education Ministry, Rumanian:
accusations from, 40, 41
budget cut by, 101
and Friendship Cup, 47
vs. Gymnastics Federation, 50–51, 78
and Onesti, 41, 47–48, 74–75
support from, 75, 77
endurance, buildup of, 199, 200
Eross, Marta, *see* Karolyi, Marta Eross
European Championships:
1975, 47–51
1977, 68–70
1979, 86

Faehn, Rhonda, 168, 182–84
and 1988 Olympic Trials, 173–75
integrity of, 182–83
as team alternate, 174–75, 178, 179, 180–81
as team backbone, 170–71

About the Authors

Bela Karolyi is an internationally acclaimed gymnastics coach who has trained champion athletes both in his native country of Rumania, as well as in his adopted homeland, America. He and his gymnasts have won ten American Cup Championships. In addition, Bela has created Olympic Champions both in his native country and his adopted homeland; his gymnasts have won over 176 medals in European and World Championships as well as the Olympic Games. He currently resides in Houston, Texas, with his wife, Marta. When not in Houston, Karolyi can be found on his ranch in New Waverly, Texas, along with his dogs, camel, llama, donkeys, steer, chickens, turkeys, raccoons, pigeons, wild pigs, and horses.

Nancy Ann Richardson is a freelance writer who has written for Ringling Bros. and Barnum & Bailey Circus, LucasArts, and the University of California, San Francisco. She currently resides in Boulder, Colorado.